I0481152

Cryptocurrency

— — — — — �& ❧ ❦ ❀ — — — — —

20 Alternatives to Bitcoin

The Smartest Way to Make Money Today

By

David Blake

express written consent from the Publisher. All additional rights reserved.

The information in the following pages is broadly considered to be a truthful and accurate account of facts, and as such any inattention, use or misuse of the information in question by the reader will render any resulting actions solely under their purview. There are no scenarios in which the publisher or the original author of this work can be in any fashion deemed liable for any hardship or damages that may befall them after undertaking information described herein.

Additionally, the information in the following pages is intended only for informational purposes and should thus be thought of as universal. As befitting its nature, it is presented without assurance regarding its prolonged validity or interim quality. Trademarks that are mentioned are done without written consent and can in no way be considered an endorsement from the trademark holder.

Table of Contents

Introduction

Congratulations on downloading *Cryptocurrency: 20 Alternatives to Bitcoin* and thank you for doing so.

There is no doubt that the cryptocurrency bandwagon has left the station and is heading for amazing destinations. The promise of great wealth is undeniable for many who may be considering investing in this new type of currency. It is exciting to be able to get in on the ground floor of any type of new investment, but there is no question that such a venture comes with its own level of risks.

Those risks are the very things that can hold a person back from making a decision to invest in cryptocurrency. The idea that it could be a fly by night operation that will soon vanish into oblivion taking your hard earned dollars with it is enough to make many hesitate. Others might be concerned that it is a scam that will one day be exposed as such or even have the idea that it is not at all what it is cracked up to be.

The reality though is pretty simple. Those are the same fears that people have wondered about in regards to any new investment opportunity. Imagine what people might have thought about Microsoft when it first announced its public offering in 1986 for a small $21/share. At that time, $21 may have seemed like a small fortune for many who took the plunge. Today, that same $21 share now sells for $84.00.

Or how about Google with its initial offering of $85/share? Even a small investment back then would have provided you with a massive windfall today. Those same shares are now being sold for over $1000. One need only look at the numbers to find big names today, like Microsoft, Google, and Amazon to see that there is high-profit potential in areas where one might least expect it.

This seems to also be the case with cryptocurrency but with a lot more reason to fear investment in this area. Unlike investing in the stock market where there are a lot of regulations and guidelines in place to protect investors and navigating the market has already been put to the test, investing in cryptocurrency is a whole new way game. Never has an innovation like this been at the disposal of so many. Investing in cryptocurrency puts you on the ground floor of a whole new way of thinking about money. From now on, money will be viewed as an investment tool in and of itself rather than a tool used to invest in other things.

So, how can you get in on this type of investment without running the risk of losing your shirt? While there is no sure-fire way to guarantee success, the key to investing in cryptocurrency lies in becoming familiar with those currencies that have set up an established track record but are still low enough in price that even those of humble means can have a chance to reap some incredible returns.

Quite often, when you mention cryptocurrency, Bitcoin comes to mind. As the first cryptocurrency introduced, it seems to be the most logical of choices as a promising investment option. However, with its price recently soaring to its highest point, ever it's quite likely already priced out of reach for most people. For them, the next best option is to find a promising alternative that will get them in on the ground floor of a potential money maker.

Unfortunately, the popularity of altcoins can be a two-edged sword. While they often promise great earnings over time, there are also many far less scrupulous individuals who are less inclined to offer you a real coin of value. They may promise you high earnings, but after a little digging, the true value of their coins will become clear.

The trick, therefore, is not in finding an altcoin to invest in. They are found nearly everywhere you look. You see them advertised on social media, on the websites you are most likely to frequent, and you may even find them marketed at your local supermarket. The reality is that as cryptocoins become more popular, you're going to find them everywhere you look. The real trick is to find a legitimate one that has the potential to become profitable over the life of your investment.

Through the pages of this book, we hope that you'll find that one little gem that can put you on the path to future wealth. It is possible if you know how to do your research and choose the right coin to invest in so you too can tap into untold profits.

How to Measure Gains

For the new investor, one of the first things they want to consider when evaluating an altcoin is the price. This makes sense for most people since they often think of cryptocurrencies in the same way as they view the stock market, but it bears mentioning that even in the whirlwind of activity on Wall Street, more needs to be considered than just a good price and the same is definitely true for this new type of venture.

A case in point, the altcoin Ripple is extremely low priced, but the potential for large gains in the future is far less likely due to their market cap of 6 billion. Because it has been around for more than five years its potential for huge returns are less likely. With more coins sold they are much closer to reaching their market cap. Still, it is holding its own as a viable coin with a long-standing future ahead of it.

Other factors you should consider is your personal crypto investment portfolio. While it may be tempting to put all your eggs in one basket, caution is definitely warranted, especially if you're looking to pick up on an initial coin offering. Things move very quickly in the crypto market, and you could win or lose big at any given time. It is therefore pertinent that you don't throw it all in on a single roll of the dice. It's best to spread your investment over a variety of coin options with the bulk of your money going into tried and proven coins.

There you have it. Those are some of the most basic guidelines for investing in cryptocurrencies. While I could spend a lot of time breaking down things in more detail for the true novice (which I attempt to do in the later chapters), there are plenty of good books out there that can already do that. With that in mind, we move on to Chapter One and discuss investment fundamentals in cryptocurrencies. After that, we get right to the meat of what you're here for. How to find the right altcoin that has the potential to be a rising star like Bitcoin and Ethereum.

So, let's get started.

Chapter 1:

What You Need to Know to Start Investing

There are several things you want to look for when you are selecting the right altcoin to invest in. As we've already mentioned, researching these coins goes far beyond the price. However, don't hesitate to factor in price if you're working with a limited budget. Still, you don't want that to be your only source of information to base your decision on. Here are a few other things you need to take a closer look at.

The Working Model

There are many coins out there for an investor to choose from. As of this writing, the number of altcoins available is well over a thousand (estimates are now well over 3000) with new ones being introduced every day. The top runners you've probably heard of are Bitcoin, Ethereum, Ripple, Litecoin, etc. However, there is a major reason why these top earners made it to the top of the list. Each one had a working plan implemented from its inception, and their development team followed through on each phase of that plan. This is a crucial element of any altcoin offered as it gives the investor a clear vision of what is expected for them to do.

As you begin to do your research on the different coins, it is important that you look for those that have a working model to review. It will be key to making sure that you are evaluating a real coin with valid prospects for future profit. With so many options you'll quickly notice that many do not have a reasonable working plan and those that do may have plans that are very vague and say very little, if anything, or real importance.

Think of it this way. How fast would you invest your money in a new business without some type of business plan in the works, without some proof that the new owners know what they're doing, or without those in positions of responsibility having proven themselves in some fashion or other? That same kind of common sense thinking is even more important when evaluating any altcoin you're considering investing in.

Who's in Charge

Next, you want to know who's really behind the altcoin. Each coin must have a development team, and each member of that team needs to show where his or her experience within the crypto world lies. In addition, they must have a respectful reputation within their field of expertise. Where did they get their experience? How do their peers view them? And what do their past accomplishments tell you? The wrong individual in charge can put a very promising altcoin on the skids before it ever has a chance to earn any money. When you invest in any type of cryptocurrency you are investing in a fast moving market, anyone without experience in the fundamentals of that market, the technological know-how, or the necessary business acumen could easily make a wrong decision, which could lead to major losses for all of their investors.

In the tried and true stock market, nothing is more important than a careful analysis of every aspect of the stock in question. The same is also true when considering investing in any type of cryptocurrency. After all, its value is only as good as the people behind it. Having a background knowledge of an altcoin's development team can shed quite a bit of light on how well the coin may do in the future.

When it comes to evaluating the development team of a particular coin, consider these factors:

- Are they backed by credibility?

- Do they actively participate in the forums, answering questions and giving additional insight into their activities?

- Do they strive to meet their deadlines and stick to the public timeline?

What is the Future of the Coin?

Here, we are not talking about in profits but in potential. The coin must have a purpose that goes well beyond the humorous ones, or the ones someone created for his great grandpappy's birthday. It has to have a wide appeal. For example, an altcoin that could only be spent in penny arcades or in amusement parks would not have as wide of an appeal as an altcoin created to be used in all sorts of shopping venues. Always look at the purpose of the coin to determine if it has a use for you.

Take a close look at the top ten altcoins listed on any exchange, and you'll notice one commonality with all of them. They have a common purpose that appeals to a large number of people who share a common interest. This is not to say that an altcoin designed to reach a smaller percentage of the population does not have profit potential. If it is well designed and created with a genuine working plan, it can have the potential to earn you a tidy little profit. However, if you're looking for the biggest gains you can get, then you want to choose those coins that can attract larger populations of people.

The Roadmap

Closely associated with the Working Plan is the roadmap for each coin. This is a section of the white paper that details exactly what steps the development team plans to take for the coin to reach its goals. It's like taking a long journey across the country. You move from A to B then to C and continue all the way down to Z with each step taking you a little closer to your goal. In the end, you receive a reward of a healthy profit.

Coins that are just out there without any working plan tend to be riskier because they show the developers have not thoroughly thought out a working plan or a definite roadmap yet. They have no idea what will happen at the next stage nor do they have any idea what r next step should be. Avoid any coin without a roadmap because any money you invest could easily find its way down the drain and end up in a vicious whirlpool from which it may never return.

Where Can You Find Them?

When a new coin is introduced, it is usually only listed on the smaller exchanges but once it has had the opportunity to gain some traction it may be picked up by some of the larger ones. This increases their exposure and thus opens the door to more trade possibilities substantially boosts their profit potential.

The Algorithm

Okay, remember when you were in Middle School, and your math teacher gave you your homework? If your teacher was like most, they weren't satisfied if you just gave them the right answer, but they were more concerned with if you **_knew how_** to find the right answer. You had to "show your work." With cryptocurrency, this is done through the use of algorithms in a process called mining.

These algorithms are computations that are used to validate every transaction as legitimate. Probably, the most commonly known is the Proof-of-Work used by Bitcoin. However, there are many other algorithms used by different coins, each created to validate the transactions specific to each coin. As you learn more about a particular coin, it would help to try to understand how the algorithms work for that currency. In addition to the Proof-of-Work, there is also the Proof-of-Stake, The Script, X11, and Cryptonight. As you learn more about these altcoins, you'll find that how their algorithms are used can make a huge difference in their success.

While it is not the topic of this book, it certainly will help you to understand your altcoin better when you understand a little about the algorithms used.

Of course, there is a lot more information that you might want to learn when it comes to investing in alternative forms of cryptocurrency but at least at this point you understand the basics. This is not one of those investments you can make without having at least a foundation of knowledge to guide you in your investment decisions. If you're like most people, you won't learn it all before you're ready to invest. Still, that is no reason why you can't earn as you learn. So, let's move on to the next chapter and take a closer look at some specific coins you might want to consider as starting options for your new cryptocurrency portfolio.

As a recap, while the price is an important factor, it is only part of the picture. As you will see, the real value is determined by:

1. The purpose of the coin

2. It's track record and potential for acceptance

3. The algorithms used

4. The market cap

5. The development team

6. And its roadmap for the future.

When all of these factors have been identified, and the answers are to your satisfaction then and only then should you consider the price of the coin and invest.

Chapter 2:

20 Altcoins Worth Considering

It is important that you recognize that all of the coins listed in this section have prices that are constantly in a state of flux so the costs you find on the exchanges could be either higher or lower than at the time of reading. Also, be sure to keep up to date and do additional research before choosing any coin to purchase. These listed here are simply examples of the potential prospects of new a rising talent in the field. With thousands to choose from, there is no limit to what you might be able to achieve. Do your due diligence just as you would in the stock market and your potential for profit can be quite high.

Verge (XVG)

**https://vergecurrency.com/langs/en/faq/
#where-can-i-go-to-learn-more-about-
verge**

Current Price: $0.0087
Market Cap: $125,407,771.70

Verge has a huge goal for the future. The development team plans to change the economic world to the point that the word Blockchain becomes as common in the household as a television or a computer. Their efforts to do that is why Verge has made it to the top of our list.

While Verge is not necessarily a new ICO, it is still relatively new. It was first introduced in 2014 and has been riding the market to the top ever since. At first glance, it appears to be just like the Bitcoin but with a few changes.

As the word cryptocurrency steadily becomes more familiar, some of the drawbacks to the new trend have become apparent. For one thing, there are some who believe in a need to incorporate a little more privacy into the transactions. This might seem strange when you consider the fact that one of Bitcoin's biggest claims is that because of the decentralized nature of cryptocurrency there is already a certain level of anonymity that is automatically built into every transaction. While this may be true, some users have met with complications, and their trades have invited even closer scrutiny because of this process. Some have reported that their accounts have been closed because they are suspected of earning their returns by illegal means and others have been accused of using the darknet for similar reasons.

Verge, on the other hand, promises that every trade will be completely untraceable while still allowing many users to be able to pay their bills through them. This is done by using something called an "Onion Router," which layers the transactions across a wide circuit. Data is encrypted at each layer of the onion before it reaches its final destination automatically making it much more difficult to trace the funds back to their original source. They also have incorporated something called an I2P integration allowing people to become hosts of servers without having to identify their location. In addition, a P2P integration gives users the option to transfer funds via a social media network. Anyone who has a presence on the same social media platform will be able to exchange funds with each other.

These special features allow Verge to circumvent many of the problems faced by Bitcoin opening the door to conducting transactions that are guaranteed to be in complete privacy. That along with working in tandem with several levels of algorithms make Verge a very promising upstart.

Their roadmap comes in three phases, developmental, social media, and exchange listings but it doesn't stop there. It is continuously being updated as they reach each of their milestones.

Promising to make transactions fast and easy for the newcomer to cryptocurrency, Verge wants to take cryptocurrency to the next level. Through them, they hope to make these types of transactions as common as paying bills online has become.

Evidence shows that it is definitely getting the recognition it seeks. Verge won an ongoing Twitter poll with close to 100,000 votes to claim its place on the HitBTC exchange the 5th largest exchange of cryptocurrencies in the entire world. Other exchanges that now include Verge include the Binance Exchange where it won the coveted title of "Coin of the Month," the Nexchange, and the Changelly. So, while Verge has already made a fine showing in many of the smaller exchanges, they are steadily infiltrating the larger exchanges proving that this is a coin that will be around for a very long time.

One other long-awaited feature to Verge is the introduction of the Wraith Protocol, which allows the user to choose between using a public and private ledger. This means that users have even more control over how to protect their private identities. This seems to be an indication of the momentum one can expect from them in the future. The Wraith Protocol is just one of many new technological additions they have planned to enhance their already strong platform for users and investors alike to look forward to.

Golem (GNT)

https://golem.network

Current Price: $0.3037
Market Cap: $253,018,475.42

The second coin on our list has also begun to take on the cryptoworld by surprise. Golem, another altcoin that is quickly propelling itself forward is now standing front and center. It, however, works a little differently. It is a currency based on the same principle as Ethereum where the value of each coin is determined by the tasks it is used to complete. Referred to as an open source, decentralized, supercomputer it gives each user the ability to connect with any other computers in the system to accomplish whatever task the user needs.

Golem, like Ethereum, can be used to perform many tasks requiring computer power but is used most often for the purposes of scientific research, data analysis, and even crypto mining. No matter how detailed, intricate, or complicated the task, using Golem connects you to a whole world of computer power to get the job done. It is so effective that it has often been referred to as the Airbnb of computers.

The process is relatively simple. Most people have computers in their homes or offices that are only using a fraction of their processing power. In the past, all of that energy would easily have gone to waste, but now, with Golem, a computer owner can literally rent out their excess computer processing power to someone else. At the same time, the individual that needs excess processing power can easily access as many computers as he needs without having to invest in a massive computer to meet his needs.

The benefits are obvious, users get access to the power needed to perform their tasks at a mere fraction of what it would cost to make such a massive investment. There is also the advantage of an added level of security as there could be no single unit that could cripple the whole computing process.

Today, people use Golem to handle functions like computer graphics, stock market analysis, determining market trends and predictions, and even to process artificial intelligence among other things.

There are several phases to the Golem roadmap. The Alpha Phase (or Brass Phase) launched in August of 2016 (the phase that introduced Golem to the world) focused purely on CGI Graphics, this is where investors could see the working model in action as well as observe how their carefully selected development team worked together. The Clay, Stone, and Iron Phases will be introduced one at a time once the coin has achieved certain milestones. It is clear that Golem has no intention of stopping or even slowing down in the near future helping investors to see the viability of potential future profits.

So, how can you the investor make money by investing in Golem? This is a logical question since the currency used is power, not money. The gains earned by using the power within the Golem Network is accumulated through fees and commissions.

The price of Golem has been steadily increasing since its inception in August of 2016 with a current price of about $0.30/coin. This can allow an investor to purchase a large sum of them before the price rises too high; something that is expected to occur sometime over the next 8-10 years.

Siacoin (SC)

http://sia.tech

Current Price: $0.0085
Market Cap: $267,198,856.86

The concept that was soon to become Siacoin first presented itself in 2013, which makes it one of the senior citizens of coins when you think about it. It came in the form of a question: what would happen if you could free up unused storage space in the virtual world and tie it all together? The answer heralded in a whole new way to look at Cloud storage. Rather than a single individual or organization holding and maintaining all the virtual storage space in the world, now every individual in the network can rent out space on their hard drive for a fraction of the cost.

Sia's decentralized network of data centers is not just more affordable than paying for traditional cloud storage, but it is also the fastest, least expensive, and most secure center in the world. This is no easy task, and their ultimate goal has yet to be reached; to be viewed in the storage world with the same name recognition as Google,

Amazon, or Apple. Their aim is basic, storage (like air) should be free, and they want to make it available to everyone they can.

As a member of the Sia platform, you can rent out storage space on your hard drive, receive payment for hosting any files you host, mine for Siacoin, or make any contribution to the program whenever you want.

As of now, Siacoin has only opened the door to basic storage capabilities, but after a closer look at their Roadmap, you quickly learn that is only the beginning for them. Just in the past year alone they have introduced such features as the ability to repair files from a remote location, reduced the amount of time needed in the Blockchain, made it possible for renters to screen and get rid of low-quality hosts, and given users the ability to use multiple wallets across several platforms.

Their long-range goals are just as impressive eventually opening the door to video streaming, sharing files with other Sia users, and the ability to recover lost files simply using your wallet seed. That and a lot more is in store for this altcoin's future.

The entire process is completely private. Sia breaks each file stored apart, encrypts it, and then sends it out over the entire decentralized platform. The only way to decrypt them is with the keys, which only the owner of the file holds. Sia owns or makes no claim to any of the data stored and no one else has access to any of these files.

It is definitely gaining in popularity as storing data is steadily becoming more and more expensive every day. For the user, the average cost of storing one terabyte of data on Sia runs approximately $2/month as compared to other cloud servers that charge $20+ for the same service.

There is no question that there is a wide range of appeal for any user that is now storing data in the cloud. As the concept of decentralization becomes more familiar, it is expected that programs like Siacoin will become the leaders of the pack in their fields of expertise and being able to get in on the ground floor of a program like this one means that you are getting in at the beginning of a major change in industry thinking.

Today, the price of Siacoin is only $0.08/coin, but one could only imagine what a healthy investment today could earn you as its popularity and reputation continues to grow.

Ripple (XRP)

**https://www.ripple.com/?gclid=Cj0KCQj
wv_fKBRCGARIsAL6R6eg01lbciDXH5EI
ViNDAtvvZB31Z4Vtv_fZ7BUc-
sk3FtrkrxiAhCYIaAnUAEALw_wcB**

**Current Price: $0.2301
Market Cap: $8,912,172,144.19**

It has often been said that we live in the
information age, but that reputation is slowly
evolving. It's just a matter of time before people
will start to say we live in the age of technology.
With all of the technological advancements, it is
no surprise that there are now houses that can
fold up and travel with you, food that can
prepare itself, and cars that do all the driving for
you.

It is in this picture of the future that Ripple
inserts itself so that everyone can benefit. It
seems that as the world continues to progress,
the system that we all use is still bogged down
with its outdated methodologies. Ripple has
plans to revamp the entire system using
decentralized technology. Their network, called
RippleNet, brings together all sorts of people,

industries, and organizations. Users will be able to connect with their bank, any businesses they make regular payments to, or even other individuals within the system and send payments seamlessly.

The system is built entirely on a scalable Blockchain that can not only provide the additional security you can't get from a centralized system but also can interconnect with other systems and adapt to them when needed. This ease of communication allows for all sorts of different transactions to take place without hassle.

It is RippleNet's flexibility that makes money transfers easy even when remitting across borders all for a fraction of the cost compared to most financial institutions in the world. Each transaction is completed in real time without a painful delay while funds are "in transit." The average time for each transaction to be completed is around 4 seconds as opposed to the Bitcoin transaction taking as much as 1-4 hours to complete.

Even that is better than many traditional financial institutions that can take days to complete a single transaction. RippleNet is prepared to take on as many as 1,500 transactions per second around the clock with the same speed, and efficiency as a credit card company does when approving purchases.

Another granddaddy when it comes to cryptocurrencies, Ripple has been around since way back in 2012 and is steadily moving forward in progress over the years. Their future goals include getting more financial institutions to join their payment system so that they can extend their reach even further. To date, they now have on board at least 11 of the world's top 100 banks and are strongly endeavoring to get more under their wings.

Today, the cost of a Ripplecoin is a small $0.23/coin with the potential for the prices to continue to increase as more and more institutions join and become active participants in their revolutionary payment system. There is much more to look forward to in the world of digital payments, and the potential for high yields on investment are still quite strong.

Maidsafe (MAID)

https://maidsafe.net/

Current Price: $0.4950
Market Cap: 224,007,795.61

Maidsafe calls itself the First Autonomous Data Network meaning that it is not a part of a corporation or organization responsible for its operations. In fact, Maidsafe works on the data scale without the need for any type of human intervention to complete its tasks. There are no stored locations, dedicated servers, or even identifiable nodes to keep the system up and running. This makes it possible for the system to function without interference. It is completely autonomous.

All this means is that once your data is stored on the Maidsafe network, it provides more security than one would expect to get from any traditional data storage facility. It is also cost-effective. Without human ideas or notions, even the fees and costs for storage are automatically computed based on available resources at the time. Prices are not set based on what someone may feel they deserve but on the actual assets on hand at the time of the transaction.

SAFE uses smart contracts and stores all data in networks specifically designed for the task. Nothing about the data storage is left to chance. Fees are calculated based on available storage space, computation time, and communication creating the perfect smart contract in the process.

The Maidsafe roadmap is introduced in three phases. Alpha I allowed users to access the system as a demonstration only platform. Alpha 2 (currently in progress) is also called the Authenticator Phase is more focused on perfecting the security across all areas of the network. Alpha 3 will add another routing layer making the entire network even more decentralized. Alpha 4 will add even more security to the storage end of the system through the reintroducing of the user run vaults so that they can access a much wider range of applications in the data storage system.

Maidsafe has a lot more in store for the future and with a price floor at around $0.49/coin at the time of this writing it is a bit higher in price than the other coins listed here. However, there is still room for the price to soar to incredible heights in the future.

NEM

https://nem.io/

Current Price: $0.2576
Market Cap: 2,318,061,243.56

NEM has goals of pushing the new blockchain technology even further than it already is. While the system is already quite impressive, NEM's goals are to take the method used to maintain a secure ledger of transactions and redesign and code them, so they are better equipped for scale and speed. By using NEM's permissioned private blockchain, they can actually produce new industry leaders in their field. This allows them to grow exponentially without losing efficiency or stability in the process.

This is all done by means of their Smart Assets System, which works to provide its users with exactly what they need. Whether a consumer needs to track the logistics of their fleet or get a document notarized their system will be able to adapt to that need. In fact, each user gets to customize the system so they can offer their professional services exactly as they want.

Users first are given a Namespace, which will in the same way as a homepage does on the Internet but instead they will be given a home on the blockchain. Then they will use a feature called Mosaics like building blocks to create the services they wish to offer. The things offered on NEM can vary widely. Businesses can offer something as simple as a coin, or something more elaborate or complicated. There is no limit to what businesses can offer. Already, this new blockchain has presented a host of solutions to countless problems that traditional centralized networks cannot compete with.

This wide range of features is possible through something called the API Gateway Server, which is used primarily to simplify the creation of the endless number of applications that are being introduced every day. Users can introduce their application in any language they choose without the need to adapt to any unfamiliar environment.

People use NEM for a wide range of reasons including transferring digital currency, creating their own digital currency, making payments, trade matching, and escrow services, some have even gone on to create their own PayPal-like system and made their own banking system.

Chapter 2: 20 Altcoins Worth Considering

Whatever your Smart Asset might be, there is a real good chance you can trade it on NEM. Their ultimate goal is to put the power of the blockchain in the hands of its users.

It is easy to see the amount of potential that an altcoin like NEM has. It opens the door to the average Joe and gives him the same power as someone with the technological know-how to set up their own blockchain and reap the benefits that come with it. This is a coin that is appealing to a wide range of people making it possible to gain huge returns in the future. With a price approaching $0.26/coin at the time of this writing, the chance to get in on the ground floor of something huge is within easy grasp of anyone who is ready to take the plunge.

Reddcoin (RDD)

https://www.reddcoin.com/

Current Price: $0.0017
Market Cap: 47,839,523.82

Another altcoin that is poised to make huge strides in the near future is the Reddcoin. With a host of additional features offered to make paying bills and purchasing goods easier than ever, it has the means to affect the way, people do business in numerous ways.

This is all done by the use of a unique algorithm that motivates people to not only want to use it but to buy into it as well. Unlike other cryptocurrencies, mining for Reddcoin requires a minimal amount of energy, so there is no need to obtain specialized equipment to do it. One can easily use their home PCs, laptops, and even mobile devices to mine for coins. Without the need for expensive equipment, Reddcoin can become a money-making tool for anyone who uses it.

It's also advantageous from the user standpoint. Their Tip Platform makes it possible to send and receive currency via the many social media platforms that are already in use by billions of people around the world.

By focusing much of their efforts on supporting transactions made through the social media platform, Reddcoin has cornered a pretty unique but massive market and is poised to reap the benefits of all that entails. Users will be able to support platforms that they regularly use by making microdonations to people or businesses of their choosing, leave tips when they want, and send money to pretty much any place on the planet for a minuscule fee that amounts to pennies compared to the traditional financial institutions.,

There are three primary goals Reddcoin has set out to accomplish. First, they want to achieve fair distribution for users, miners, and investors. Second, they are seeking to enhance their algorithm so that they have a more secure network that encourages more use, ownership, and investment opportunities, and finally, they are steadily working to build up their decentralized network in such a way as to attract even more talent and skilled people to join their development team.

Clearly, this is an altcoin well worth considering as an investment tool. And with the current price trading at $0.001/coin it is the ideal time to invest. As we have all seen the way the majority of the world has embraced social media, Reddcoin looks to one day be right at the forefront of it all. A perfect and ideal opportunity to get in on the ground floor of something that has the potential to be grow exponentially in the very near future.

Voxels (VOX)

https://www.voxelus.com/

Current Price: $0.2668
Market Cap: 56,026,971.90

Now there is even an altcoin for gamers! Voxel allows anyone, regardless of their location, to access online games and create, share, or play them in virtual reality. Regardless of whether you're just a faithful gamer or a full-time developer, the potential here is quite high.

We all know that gaming is big business and virtual reality is almost bigger than life. With Voxel opening the door for players to become more actively involved in the development process the coin could have a wide appeal globally. Now, rather than just play in an exciting new virtual world, you can also help to create the game you're playing, adding your own features to a new fantasy, something that no one had even thought about. There is no need to learn any technical coding language or have any unique and special skills to be a part of this virtual world.

While they have already made huge strides in the field of gaming, they have much more in store. Very soon, users will be allowed to collaborate together on creating whole new games and creating awesome virtual reality features without the need for specialized equipment. You can look through thousands of gaming features offered on their website that have been made available by other users and repurpose them to be used in your game development strategy.

With Voxel, you also get real time multiplayer support for any of the games you create or play. It stands to be a very exciting altcoin for anyone who is serious about online gaming. Voxel is taking virtual reality games to an entirely new level, and it is definitely going to be the altcoin of choice for anyone who wants to be a part of this technological world.

Why is this so exciting? There are lots of places where gamers can become more actively involved in their games. But Voxel users do not have to have any technical knowledge or experience in designing, coding, to be able to contribute to the creation of these virtual worlds.

This is because their technology is truly unique. In most other gaming programs, the GPUs have been designed to support polygons, but with Voxel tech, users have access to a tool that allows them to create more than a virtual reality experience but in a form that is "photorealistic" imagery as well. This is not another version of the same old games that people are playing today, but it is instead, the very future of virtual reality.

With today's price a mere $0.21/coin, the opportunities to grow your investment are very high. The altcoin exudes possibilities, and if you're serious about gaming, this will probably be the area where you are most likely inclined to invest your money. There is a lot more in store for Voxel so it is one of those altcoins that investors should watch very closely. By doing so, it will be easy to follow the constant stream of new additions and releases to the gaming world.

Bitbay (BAY)

https://bitbay.market/

Current Price: $0.0785
Market Cap: 79,144,702.10

For those looking for an altcoin that allows for a more practical approach to shopping then the Bitbay coin may be your best choice. Bitbay is specifically designed to facilitate purchases and transactions without hassles. Its focus is on the use of Smart Contract technology that when created is literally impossible to break yet entirely enforceable. These contracts allow for peer to peer currency exchanges without the use of a middleman thus eliminating large service fees for every transaction made.

Those who use BitBay will never have to worry about funds getting seized because every transaction is peer-to-peer without any form of third-party reporting. There is no threat of their funds being stolen because of its tight security. It also eliminates the need for person-to-person meetings or long, drawn out escrow periods. They have even installed a unilateral "Guarantor" contract that makes it possible for sellers to let in new buyers without requiring a deposit. This way it is easy for anyone to buy or sell with BitBay.

Other features BitBay offers are the "Deadman's Switch," which allows for users to have their coins returned to them under certain conditions specified in the contract. They also have something called a "Notary and Burn" feature, which can be used to verify ownership of products or coins. These and many other features are what gives BitBay a strong future in the cryptoworld.

Introduced in 2014, BitBay has a lot more in store for its users in the future. There are several new "surprise releases" they plan to introduce over the next year that will help to propel the coin even further in the crypto community. With anti-theft features, multisignature wallets, Tor and proxy options, decentralized voting, exotic spending, and double deposit escrows BitBay seems to be offering much more in terms of features than any other altcoin designed for shopping.

Considered to be the first in the world to offer a fully-functional and decentralized marketplace.

BitBay's unique technology has the power to put everyone in their own business, sell their goods and services and remain completely anonymous in the process. Once the deal is done, they can collect their earnings and move right on to their next customer.

We all know that cryptocurrency is about to change the way we shop forever but with all the extras BitBay offers, it is certainly exciting to be able to get in on the ground floor of this burgeoning operation. With a small cost of $0.08/coin the potential for major earnings is very high and its future is very bright.

NXT (NXT)

https://nxtplatform.org/

Current Price: $0.6178
Market Cap: 617,228,387.75

The NXT altcoin builds on the platform originally set up with Bitcoin. The advanced, open-sourced blockchain provides numerous core-level features like a Decentralized Asset Exchange, its own marketplace, and a voting system. The platform is exotic enough to avoid common problems other cryptocurrencies may have to deal with. For example, restriction to a particular payment system is not possible. Users can also create their own marketplace listings without fear of being denied, and developers can create their own applications through the program interface.

The program's core features are many including, peer-to-peer exchanges of currency, their own monetary system, marketing, messaging, account control, coin shuffling, data cloud, and a whole lot more.

Unlike other cryptocurrencies that rely heavily on the platform laid out by Bitcoin when it first introduced cryptocurrency to the world, NXT is different. Users can create their own applications right on the blockchain giving them the freedom to use their currency as they see fit. They have complete control over the way the currency is used as well as when and where.

There is no limit to how or who a user can trade with, and there is literally no reason fear that a transaction could be denied based on some guidelines set by someone else. Through NXT you can even create your own tokens to trade over the Asset Exchange Platform. Users can also set up their own crowdfunding projects, implement their own tools to verify the authenticity of any transactions and get a world of support for a new and more modern way of doing business.

Developers even have the capability of creating their own nodes within the system or creating their own software programs to get whatever task is needed to be done. Since it is an open-sourced platform, anyone who wants to contribute to its development is welcome. Being a part of this new and innovative form of cryptocurrency means that you are a part of an ever-changing environment. As it grows, so will your interests.

As the economic scene continues to evolve, predictions indicate that altcoins that can be adapted to a constantly changing environment are the ones most likely to excel. Users and investors alike will benefit greatly once they grasp the importance of how these types of coins will continue to be used over the long term. Today, with a price set at $0.41/coin there is plenty of room for the kind of growth you can look forward to seeing in the very near future.

Dogecoin (DOGE)

http://dogecoin.com/

Current Price: $0.0027
Market Cap: 304,438,408.25

The Dogecoin is an altcoin with many features. It gives the user the ability to buy goods and services, make trades for other currencies, and can be used in much the same way that one might use the traditional paper money. One feature that is very popular is the "tipping" feature that allows you to send a microtip to those who create or share online content with other Dogecoin users. When you appreciate something, you've read online and rather than "liking" it you can now give the writer a monetary reward that has real value.

They currently have plans to place a widget on Facebook so friends can "tip" each other for anything they consider to be a job well done. Through Doge, you can donate to organizations, reward others that have done great things for others, or just contribute to projects struggling to get started.

Its popularity has been propelled to the forefront by a large support community that is spreading the word rapidly. As evidence of its wide range of support, the average uptrend of most altcoins is around 20%, but the Dogecoin upward movement has soared up a whopping 250%. It is a strong indication that Dogecoin is getting a much wider recognition mainly for its more noble causes than one that is there only for monetary value. It can be very exciting to see how philanthropy in action can be of benefit to just about everyone involved.

Whether you purchase your Dogecoins outright or you earn them through microtips, they can be used to make purchases online. You can buy goods or services, trade them for other cryptocurrencies, or even save them as an investment tool. However, if you're like the rest of the people in the Dogecoin community, you won't need to spend a lot of time searching for a place that will take them.

Dogecoin was originally designed as a spoof off of the often too serious investors of Bitcoin. The developers wanted to create something with a little more fun and a lot more tongue in cheek kind of action but were surprised to learn that many people actually liked the idea. Today, many people are joining the Dogecoin community and are being richly rewarded for it. With a current price at $0.002/coin, getting in on a ground floor opportunity can be more than exciting with lots of potential for growth for any new investor.

Digibyte (DGB)

https://digibyte.io/

Current Price: $0.0161
Market Cap: 153,690,234.32

Digibyte is one of the fastest growing cryptocurrencies out there. One of the reasons for this rapid growth is its highly advanced technology that enables transactions to be completed in a matter of seconds. Their digital assets are so secure they can never be destroyed, hacked, or illegally duplicated. Counterfeiting Digibyte coins is virtually impossible ensuring that every transaction you make is a valid one. This makes them the perfect tool for transferring assets like data, currency, and even property.

The program is completely decentralized, and their blockchain is quite extensive covering more than 100,000 separate computers, mobile devices, servers, and nodes spread around the globe. They use five separate highly advanced algorithms to prevent the chances of any centralized mining taking place, and they have several layers of adjustments in place to avoid the risk of any form of crypto attacks or attempts at hacking. This high level of security means they have been capable of fixing 90% of the vulnerabilities that all financial institutions have to deal with. This type of security is also what sets it apart from so many other cryptocurrencies on the market.

Since its launch in early 2014, Digibyte has become such a popular coin that it now boasts the longest blockchain in history with more than 5 million blocks to speak of. Their goals continue to expand so that ultimately, they hope to reach even further into the crypto community.

One thing that makes Digibyte unique is that they have never had an ICO. It seems the coin hit the ground running and has not slowed down since. With no presale, token sale, or any of the other common introductory tactics Digibyte has made its own name and is moving quickly towards greater and greater profits. This is mainly due to its large community of supporters, their technologically advanced development team, and the scalable algorithms that are constantly at work. Their ultimate goal is to match the speed and accuracy of VISA within the next three years.

Another reason for its vast popularity is its non-profit status that is dedicated to contributing funds to three core areas of interest, education, outreach, and development. From these three core areas, the development team creates and funds numerous projects designed to advance expertise in each of these areas.

There are many ways you can use Digibyte coins, but it was created primarily for the purpose of making digital payments within the cyber world ensuring that funds are protected through every channel of the process.

The cost of a Digibyte coin today is still hovering at the $0.01/coin mark, so the potential for great strides to be had are quite high. Anyone looking to invest in an altcoin with a promising future will do well to seriously take the time to sit down and study the possibilities here.

Stella Lumens (XLM)

https://www.stellar.org/lumens/

Current Price: $0.1492
Market Cap: 2,660,511,714.24

The Stella Lumens coin allows you to transmit funds across borders without the aid of a middleman. This saves on a host of fees and an expenditure of valuable time while you wait for other institutions to validate transactions. While it is very similar to other decentralized programs, Stella Lumens sets itself apart through something called integration. This is a process that allows your computer systems to speak directly with other computer systems within the network to identify the use case that is best suited to the type of transaction you want to perform.

Once that is determined, the network will set up databases unique to your needs, write the necessary code, conduct the transaction, and then test to make sure that your transaction was completed correctly. This adds an additional layer of security for anyone sending money to other countries. With this detailed strategy, the sender can be assured that the recipient not only gets the funds he needs but receives them in their preferred form of currency and at the lowest possible rate.

The entire system is basically free to use however, there is a nominal fee paid by the sender of each transaction (.00001 XLM, the equivalent of a fraction of a fraction of a penny) so whether you're a private person sending money to a family member or you're a large corporation sending payroll to employees overseas, the cost to use their service is considered to be without fee. Stella is a non-profit foundation dedicated to connecting people to low-cost financial services especially in areas where many people are financially disadvantaged. Since there are no fees dedicated to each transaction, the system is funded entirely by tax-deductible donations from the public and their users.

With a large number of the world population without access to traditional banking services and the cost of such services out of reach of many, the attraction of Stella Lumens is unmistakable. The chances for huge profits as the coin continually increases in value is well within reach. To add to its appeal, Stella Lumens is even preparing to introduce a low-bandwidth option for those who do not have regular or fast Internet usage. This will enable them to still send and receive monies without the use of a regular Internet connection opening the door to many more possibilities.

Today, the price of a single Stella Lumens coin is a mere $0.11/coin making it easy to get in on this type of investment.

STEEM (STEEM)

https://www.stellar.org/lumens/

Current Price: $1.93
Market Cap: 474,597,973.83

Considered to be a "Smart Media Token," STEEM coins are used to monetize online content with the purpose of encouraging a desired behavior. Now, with so much information flooding the online market, it is becoming more and more difficult for both those who create content and those who publish it to make a profit. In the past, businesses could earn money via online advertising, but with the increased usage of ad blockers, that possibility is quickly becoming less viable.

STEEM however, hopes to resolve that issue and get money to the people that are truly working for it. Each STEEM token allows publishers to build up a following in support of his or her own online community based on the economic incentives offered. With near-zero transaction fees, publishers and creators alike can even do their own fundraising encouraging microdonations to support their cause. Each token purchased can be used to send a reward via a small micropayment to their creator or publisher of choice. The more tokens received, the higher the incentive to continue producing that kind of material for the public. Today, many platforms social media platforms like Facebook are happy to skim off of the profits of those who use their page yet they rarely are as giving when sharing any revenues they may have accumulated. STEEM allows creators to bypass this type of market and receive funds directly for the work they do.

STEEM offers two types of tokens, the posting rewards, and the curation rewards. The posting rewards tokens are designed so that the user can give them to anyone they find on the Internet that is producing material that is appealing to them and the curation rewards, which are meant to be distributed to creators that receive the most upvotes in any particular area.

There is no fee attached to each transaction and publishers can align themselves with any number of their supported platforms. Once they are set up, there is no additional skill or knowledge they need. They can then focus their attention on providing the kind of quality content their followers are looking to learn about.

There are several ways publishers can generate their own source of revenue through STEEM. They can use single token support where they can design and create their own coins and generate income, they can use the multiple token support where public forums can generate income by tapping into a specific niche of some kind, or they can create a comments widget that allows them to collect tokens based on the comments received.

As more and more people are spending their lives on the world-wide-web, it is clear that rewarding publishers, creators, and even commenters for their participation can mean a great deal for all those involved. With many governments lagging behind in regulating content, this is one way to manage content so that information that does not have wide appeal will find itself struggling for revenue while the more popular sites will continue to grow and prosper.

It has caught on so well that in the past year, STEEM has sent out nearly $23 million in rewards for quality online content and is expected to pay out even more over the next year. With each token priced at $1.49/coin, it still has room to grow many times over in the next few years.

Neblio (NEBL)

https://nebl.io/wallets/

Current Price: $4.14
Market Cap: 52,180,261.01

Neblio is the altcoin specifically designed for businesses. The coin was developed to overcome some early obstacles with businesses adopting the new blockchain technology. To be successful, they had to figure out a way to factor in a business' need for transparency, reliability, and security something that the blockchain was already designed to do. Once they accomplished that the possibilities for success were phenomenal. Yet, still many companies were reluctant to cash in on the unproven strategies they had developed.

Neblio has set out to streamline the process making it considerably easier to tailor it to each business' particular needs. A prime example could be seen with a doctor's office needing to have access to certain patient data. With a centralized data system, the information would all be contained on a single server with the constant risk of a break in access at a point when the data was most needed. However, with Neblio's plan to tailor the blockchain to each user's unique needs, all the patient data can be contained on the blockchain without exposure to the usual risks being hacked, server downtime, or any exposure to loss. Neblio can adjust their blockchain to support all manner of businesses in such a way that it is more appealing for them to use them over the traditional centralized servers that many are now relying on.

In addition, their roadmap includes plans to eventually adopt all forms of programming languages in the future so that no business will be forced to relearn or dedicate time to developing new processes to become a part of the cryptocurrency network thus making it much simpler for them to become part of the new economic revolution that is happening today.

Through Neblio, there will be a blockchain designed to cater to every business' unique needs. It will be scalable without any point of weakness where a potential failure can happen. Their platform is completely intuitive so that it can even predict whatever the new business' needs are and automatically begin to develop a way of managing that need.

Each token used on the Neblio blockchain can easily be shared with other Neblio users. This coin is definitely an early riser born less than a year ago, it is already many times more than the value of its initial coin offering. As of this writing, it is selling at just over $4, which is astronomical considering that it has only been on the market for ten months at this point.

There is much to look forward to in the world of Neblio, and anyone who is sincerely interested in the one coin that is doing everything it can to bring more business enterprise into the blockchain will do well to do a little more research to see just how fast they can get a larger return on their investment.

Bytom (BTM)

https://bytom.io/

Current Price: $0.1908
Market Cap: 188,327,467.63

Bytom is another coin that is currently on the fast track to the top. Born in China, its whitepaper explains its purpose; to serve as an intermediary that can be used to bring together generalized blockchains with those that are more specialized. It has sometimes been described as a true sleeper coin due to its similarities to the American made NEM but coming from a very different and highly unexpected place.

Its format consists of three separate layers, data transactions and transmissions, contract, and asset interaction, each with its own role and purpose designed to enhance the strength of the coin itself. To put it more simply, the power of Bytom is to take an offline asset and be able to register and trade it on the Blockchain. This means that it can serve as a bridge connecting the two separate worlds together. This way, physical currency and digital currency can all be traded on the same platform regardless of its nature. This is a feature that to date, no other coin on the market has tried to offer.

This unique position is a testament to why the coin has so quickly gained traction and is poised to do great things in the very near future. Their roadmap outlines their goals, giving investors a clear view of exactly what to expect and when. Based on their team's own predictions many new things are slated to be introduced at the beginning of 2018 with much more expectations later on. This puts Bytom in a unique position where in the world of cryptocurrency, for the moment, they have no clear competition in their area of expertise. This leaves a wide open space where profits can escalate astronomically before someone else decides to join them in a healthy competition.

Bytom is primarily found on the Chinese exchanges, but westerners can now purchase tokens through the Cryptopia exchange. This means they are still not listed on any major coin exchanges but at least now anyone who lives in the western world can have easy access to purchasing them.

Those who choose to invest in Bytom gain profit by holding shares on the actual blockchain. Its profits come entirely from the fees each user pays to have access to its massive network of nodes. Currently, trading at $0.13/coin, Bytom is expected to make huge strides forward in the next few months. At this price, it is the perfect time to buy in before the big surge is expected in the very near future.

TRON (TRX)

https://tronlab.com/en.html

Current Price: $0.0041
Market Cap: 272,157,190.95

Tron is another currency that is looking to literally change the way we do things. Their goal to develop a global, free content, entertainment system is destined to attract a lot of interest. Headed by Justin Sun, one of Forbes Asia 30 under 30 he seems to have his finger on the pulse of the future of business with the next generation.

The protocol is surprisingly basic, each user can freely publish and store his or her own data on the blockchain and then decide how to distribute it to other users. They may opt to offer their digital content on a subscription basis or by offering it in tandem with other digital assets as a package. Whatever is decided, the universal applications are immense.

One of the biggest groups to follow them are the gamers. This is mainly due to a few blips in other gaming programs that have caused no little amount of frustration. A perfect example of this is the pay-to-win microtransactions that gamers often want to invest in. In the present model, gamers can accumulate assets in one game only to discover they cannot transfer those assets to their next game. This could translate into a highly expensive venture that could cost them hundreds of dollars. When it is all over, there are very few opportunities for them to sell those assets to other users or to cash out on their investment. In addition to that, if they choose to switch to another game, they usually have to enter a new game from the very beginning and build up their assets all over again. It can be a vicious cycle that could end up costing a lot of money.

However, Tron promises to change all of that. Not only will gamers be able to transfer their assets from other games, but they will also be able to generate income from their content in much the same way YouTube users generate income from the content they upload.

Tron has a uniquely designed development team consisting of members that wholeheartedly believe that protocol, from its very inception, is an asset for all people and not merely a tool used to benefit a few. For that reason, they created a non-profit organization solely dedicated to operating the entire network with a transparent, fair, and open platform in mind.

The foundation is based in Singapore and therefore is governed by their Accounting and Corporate Regulatory Authority. This automatically gives Tron a level of stability as Singapore has long been recognized for its stable and well-established laws governing their financial environment. The government, however, has no invested interest in the foundation, so any profits gained by the network is considered surplus and belongs entirely to the foundation, which is to be set aside and used for the implementation of any new additions or features to the Tron network.

There are four basic characteristics of the Tron protocol. First, Data Liberation, which allows for all data to be distributed freely without charge. Content Enabling allows for digital assets to be obtained through the spread of those contents. Personal ICO: any user is permitted to distribute their contents via an ICO while other users are still able to access and use the same digital assets. And finally a completely decentralized infrastructure.

Tron's future seems to be all but set with very few drawbacks. Still, how fast they grow and succeed will depend largely on how easily other gamers will adopt their transparent and free for all platform and how many gamers will gravitate to them over the other already proven platforms. There is no question that Tron has the potential to be a multi-billion dollar network if all their cards are played well. And now with the price at the time of this writing set at $0.0046, the potential for major growth still lies in its future. This is definitely an altcoin worth watching over the months to come.

Rise (RISE)

https://rise.vision/index.php#whatisrise

Current Price: $0.4438
Market Cap: 50,211,659.45

For any new business start-ups, it would be well worth your while to take a closer look at RISE. At its very core, this altcoin provides users with Smart Contracts and side-chain token creation covering many of the challenges new businesses have to deal with. All of this is powered by a PdoS blockchain, a network of nodes managed by 101 delegates specifically chosen by the RISE committee.

Its basic function is to offer a tailored ecosystem for businesses, investors, and tech users that is completely void of a centralized middle institution. Their ultimate goal is to draw away many users from competitor platforms by making Software Development Kits available to new users. Through these kits, anyone will be able to use RISE regardless of the computer language they use or their preferred system. Their applications can be run on Windows, MAC, or LINUX and the kits can use JavaScript,

Python, or Ruby. There is also a kit that allows for users to be able to pool their resources even when their own equipment is not compatible.

One feature that is of major appeal to many is their Blockchain Incubator used for new Decentralized Applications. Any developer creating a new start-up Dapp will be able to use the RISE platform to create their new businesses or tokens. All RISE holders are automatically entitled to share 20% of any coins developed in the incubator when the product does finally launch. While RISE is not the first altcoin to make this type of offer, getting a 20% stake in any future business is pretty high in comparison to the other tokens available now.

So far, there are two businesses that have successfully used RISE's Blockchain Incubator. The first is a company called Interlet, which is poised to compete with Airbnb. Their goal is to cut out the expensive middleman fees charged by Airbnb and pass the savings onto the consumer. The second is an online casino platform that is slated to be launched in early 2018 called Chipz. When it does launch, any RISE holders will automatically be given a percentage of Chipz tokens based on the percentage of RISE they hold at the time. The good news is that once those tokens are received, users will be available to cash them in for fiat currency at any point even if they don't have any desire to participate in the casino games offered.

RISE has several projects waiting to be launched over the next year, so there is a lot more to look forward to in the very near future. This includes the launch of a new mobile-friendly app so that users will be able to navigate their investments on the fly.

They also have a pretty strong team behind all of their future plans. Each of their ten members has a long history in the cryptoworld and has a lot to offer in bringing this new altcoin to fruition. With this type of support and a rapidly growing community, RISE has a very popular future. Already trading at $0.44/coin they seem to be on the fast track to rising stardom and anyone that chooses to become a part of the trend is expected to see some positive returns very soon.

Funfair (FUN)

https://funfair.io/

Current Price: $0.0336
Market Cap: 142,802,553.50

Ready to turn the online gaming industry on its ear is the Funfair coin. These ERC 20 tokens use Smart Contracts to execute all sorts of transactions. Their ultimate goal is to capitalize on the ever-growing $40+ billion online casino industry, a major industry that is expected that to double in size over the next few years. That opens the door to all sorts of growth potential for FUN.

Their aim is to help facilitate the development of more online casinos found in the cyber world, especially those that can offer 3-D games developed with HTML5 and other new technologies. These new games will be available at a considerably lower cost for users and therefore will naturally attract more players.

FUN games will also be more attractive as each one will be set up using Smart Contracts so there will be no question as to fairness in play. Transparency will be clear as every function will be publicly displayed on the blockchain, so it will be evident that the games will not be heavily slanted towards the house in any way. This in itself will attract a lot of new players as they come to realize that the results of the games are truly random.

While there have definitely been other online gaming casinos in the cryptoworld, FUN hopes to overcome some of the obstacles that others have experienced. The need for more direct and immediate payouts, the lack of regulation, and the constant fluctuations in the value of the currency have all had a negative impact on the online gaming industry. However, with FUN's development team working to overcome these issues. Their extensive background in the gaming world and their expertise in technology, they are implementing several new features that will directly address those issues.

The platform plans to bring game developers, casino operators, and players all together in one place in a simple, more efficient, and a fun way to exchange ideas. Already they have a wide range of prototype games available with the hopes of a full-scale launch in the very near future.

Cryptocurrency: 20 Alternatives to Bitcoin

Already a winner in its own right, it has recently earned the ICO coin of the year at the iMalta Gaming Awards, FUN is on the fast track to success. And their plans to introduce many more award-winning games within the next few months is definitely enough to warrant the attention of any investors.

It is important that you fully understand that their success is not expected to be tied solely to one casino but that of thousands. So, once an online casino chooses to adopt the FUN platform, they will join a host of others in generating revenue that will be shared among all the holders of FUN tokens. This has of course, not come without its own obstacles but the FUN developers are constantly at work to improve the transaction times and other challenges that are common among online casinos.

While there is no doubt that there are still quite a few bugs to be worked out in relation to the online gaming industry, the FUN development team is steadily working to overcome these obstacles so that they can provide one of the most rewarding online casino experiences a player could have. This translates into a high potential for profit for both users and token holders alike. Over the next few months, you can fully expect to see many more innovative ideas being released by FUN so there will always be something to look forward to.

With their aim to capitalize on the global online gaming industry one can expect a very high return on their investment. At the time of this writing, FUN tokens are trading at $0.0333/coin leaving a lot of room to grow for the avid gamer.

OKCash (OK)

http://okcash.io/#aboutPage

Current Price: $0.6005
Market Cap: 44,068,314.16

Running under the slogan, "the future of cash," OKCash is a platform that promises to ease the ability to make microtransactions online. Their goal to operate a global payment system eliminating cross-border transaction fees and near instant validation times has the potential to tap into a major part of this market.

Their low-cost fees open the door to all sorts of microtransactions that can include tipping and donating making it possible for exchanges of money that would otherwise never occur because of the exorbitant fees associated with traditional methods of cross-border exchanges. The transparency of each transaction being made public and the ability to make donations via social media channels makes the whole process faster and easier than ever before.

While there are several other altcoins that allow for these types of transactions, what gives OKCash its strongest appeal is the extremely low-cost fees they charge, falling even below other altcoins. At the time of this writing, the fees were listed at 0.0001 to send and no fee to receive any funds sent to you. In the overall world of cross-border transactions, this is unheard of.

In addition, OKCash also offers an extra level of privacy with their built-in encrypted technology. This ensures that every transaction made will remain completely confidential with virtually no risk of their identity ever being revealed or uncovered.

As evidence of its growing popularity, in its early months, OKCash saw more than 136,000 OK wallets created holding more than 1000 OKCash tokens. Part of the reason for this is their proof-of-stake mining algorithm, which tends to use much less energy than those coins that use the original proof-of-work algorithm. With their new model, anyone who wants to can participate in the OKCash network.

Another exciting feature of the OKCash network is their team's focus on the online video game industry. While this is a newer aspect of the OK coin, investors can fully expect that there will be many more similar projects to look forward to in the future.

Currently, OKCash boasts to have the lowest transaction fees on the market, built-in protection against fraud, some of the fastest transactions in the world, and the ability to accept credit cards to complete different transactions. It is fast becoming a globally recognized means of sending funds across borders. In time, it is expected to become a world recognized means of transferring funds that will give people everywhere an affordable means of sending money around the globe.

It is easy to understand how OKCash will continue to grow over the coming years. Today, it is trading at a value of $0.57/coin, and it is steadily growing. No one knows exactly how far OKCash will continue to grow, but it does appear that it shows no evidence of slowing down anytime in the near future.

It is important to point out that OKCash is not to be confused with OKCash.cn, a Chinese based cryptocurrency that uses Bitcoin instead of its own altcoin.

Chapter 3:

Buyer Beware

The world of cryptocurrency is an exciting one, and as more and more people become familiar with this new means of earning a profit, there will be plenty of opportunities to make money for everyone, but there will also be plenty of ways to lose it as well. It is important to note that many of the losses people experience when investing in altcoins can be avoided with just a little bit of understanding of how the system works.

In this chapter, we're going to look a little closer at some of the most common pitfalls that many new investors make and how to avoid them so that you can get the most out of their investment.

Do Your Own Research

There is nothing wrong with getting someone's opinion about what may be a promising coin for the future. As a matter of fact, there are many professional investors in other markets who do exactly that. However, the most successful of these investors will never put all of their hard earned money into any instrument without doing their own research.

As you talk to more and more people about cryptocurrency, you'll often hear and see comparisons made to the stock market. While there are some similarities, there are some very distinct differences you need to keep in mind.

1. Cryptocoins do not represent corporations. They represent the value of the currency used within a specific network. That value is determined not by the amount of revenue they generate but rather by their acceptance within a given community.

2. Cryptocurrency is new. All cryptocurrencies are new and therefore are all in the developmental stage. That fact alone means that there is a higher level of risk that even successfully performing coins are going to experience. Therefore, many of them will lack a strong track record you can follow to pick out trends and behaviors.

Just understanding those two fundamental factors should encourage you to take your research on these coins very seriously. It is not just an investment of your money, but it will require an investment in time as well. In addition, it is imperative that we conduct our research with these other factors in mind. Before we invest, we need to understand how the coin will operate and at the very least, the technological function of the algorithms and languages used in its operations. While most of us do not have that kind of technological mind, a visit to each coin's website will usually have the process broken down in simple layman's terms so that you can better grasp what the coin does at its core.

Here are just a few basic steps that can help you to navigate the world of cryptocurrency and research coins on your own.

The Whitepaper: The first thing you should look at is the coin's whitepaper. This is a proposal written by the coin's development team that gives you a basic understanding of the coin's purpose and the simple mechanics. This should be the primary tool you'll use for evaluating the validity of any coin.

The Coin's community forum or blog: Blogs, forums, and chat groups dedicated to the coin will be your primary resource to help you to understand how the public sees the coin's performance. It's your way of getting the pulse of the community surrounding it. This is especially important if you found the information in the whitepaper too technical for you to grasp. These are usually open forums where you can get your questions answered or explanations broken down into a plain and simple language. A common acronym you'll find on these forums is "ELI5," which basically means, "explain it to me like I was 5-years-old," a term most people find useful when they begin to research cryptocoins.

Have a checklist: As you learn more and more about cryptocurrency, you'll be able to develop your own checklist of things to know before making your investment. This should be a number of systematic questions you need answers to before you decide to invest in any coin. However, for the novice investor who may not know what questions to ask just yet, here are a few suggestions to get you started:

1. Market Cap: should be over 1 million

2. Number of followers on Twitter (minimum 5,000+ is a good threshold)

3. Has already created a Slack channel

4. Website is running SSL (https)

5. Easy to find roadmap

6. Information about members is easily accessible

7. Included on a number of different exchanges

8. High and steady daily trading volume (+10.00)

9. Well-designed and easily navigable website

10. Purpose of the coin is unique and sets it apart from other similar altcoins

Things that could serve as a warning sign.

1. No recent blog updates (6 months or more)

2. No recent social media updates (1 month or more)

3. Website is not functioning

4. Links to website do not work

5. Nothing sets it apart from other altcoins

6. Staking rewards are too high

7. Watch out for premining

8. The wallet is not syncing

9. Development team is too small

10. Registration is not working

11. Wallet only available for Windows. Nothing set up for OX/Linux or other platforms

Of course, these are just some simple guidelines when it comes to research. As you become more familiar with what to expect, you will develop your own list of things to watch for as you learn more.

Chapter 4:

Where to Get Your Information

After carefully looking at the coin's whitepaper and website there are a few other places where you can dig a little deeper for more information. After all, no coin is going to come right out and tell you about the potential downfalls it may face. For that, you may have to look elsewhere to balance the scales.

The Slack Channel

This is the open line of communication between members of the development team. Once you join this channel, you'll be kept up to date on all of the developments, challenges, or other events that could affect the price or advancement of the coin. Once you join, feel free to consider yourself part of the coin family and don't hesitate to ask questions, voice your concerns, or share your opinion in a way that matters. Chances are if you've thought about it someone else also has the same concerns.

Community Forums

There are quite a few public forums you can join that can get your unanswered questions answered. Forums like Bitcointalk, Reddit, and Steemit all will likely have a page on the coin you're considering. Aside from getting your questions answered, these sites can be very useful in giving you other perspectives of a coin that you may not have considered yourself. It is a way to get a well-rounded view of a coin and how it is impacting the general public as a whole.

Get Specific

When evaluating a coin, don't be afraid to get specific. Remember that all coins must be designed with a specific purpose in mind. A coin that merely mimics another coin is not going to have a lot of appeal to the public. Make sure that it solves a real problem, one that affects a large population of people otherwise there won't be enough incentive for people to use it.

Is it Understandable?

By its very nature, cryptocurrency is highly technical. However, if you're reading the whitepaper and you find it is full of technical jargon or lots pumped-up marketing phrases without telling you much of anything concrete it is usually a tool to cover up the fact that the coin really has no solid basis with which to build on. It's generally best to avoid a lot of colorful terminologies or technical jargon that really only adds fluff to the underlying message. A true coin of value will stand out on its own without the need of colorful speech to dress it up.

Who's Backing it?

Find out who's backing the coin. Start with your knowledge of the development team and their background, it won't take long looking through the forums and the blogs to find out who is throwing in with the coin. Big name investors and those with a lot of technical know-how and foresight can tell you a lot about the coin and where it's going. You want a coin that is going someplace? Look for well-known investors, and you're most likely tapping into a winner.

Learn the Terminology

It helps a lot to learn the proper technology connected with the coin. You'll often find within a description of the particular coin terms like "Proof-of-Work," and "Proof-of-Stake" used quite often. These terms are often at the core of how the coin operates and how to determine its value. While this jargon may be challenging for some people, understanding them is at the very heart of understanding the coin and how it is supposed to function.

Study the Roadmap

Just as important as understanding how a coin is supposed to work, its purpose, and its development team are knowing exactly where it plans to go in the future. No coin with a high potential of profits has plans to stay put. The cryptoworld is growing at a rapid pace, and those that are not continuously pushing forward will soon find themselves falling far behind. As more and more coins are being introduced, the competition for a successful coin is becoming fierce.

The coin's roadmap should be more than a list of what they plan to do, it should also detail the how and when these things will be introduced. This can be a powerful indication that the development team is serious about the success of the coin and not just its potential for making money.

Conclusion

So, there it is. The cryptocurrency world is an exciting one; one that promises a host of wealth and fortune for the right investor. As long as you know how to do your own research, what to look for, and what to expect there is no reason why you can't join an already long line of investors who have already made a windfall in this highly lucrative field.

It cannot be stressed enough that the coins listed in this book were promising considerations at the time of this writing but may not be at the time of your reading. It is therefore imperative that you check each coin out for yourself by following the links included to each coin's particular website. As you research make sure that you follow the checklist we've included and get all the answers to your questions before you make a decision.

We do not in any way, endorse any of these coins as a guaranteed investment tool but simply list them as having potential. If you follow through as we've suggested, we're sure you'll be that much closer to the ideal investment coin to add to your financial portfolio.

One final point we want to discuss before closing. Always, always, always make sure that there are no scam warnings or legal issues in relation to any coin you are considering. All cryptocurrencies are by nature decentralized, which should automatically set them apart from other investment tools. Be careful as some coins may claim to be cryptocurrencies but are based on an MLM structure. Cryptocurrencies should always be decentralized, and anything other than that is not a true cryptocoin. If it does not say decentralized, then you can be pretty sure that it is a scam and you should avoid it at all costs.

The world of cryptocurrency is not just a fly by night operation that will be here today and gone tomorrow. It has the potential of turning the world's economic stage on its head and will literally change the way we view currency. We are living in exciting times with much to look forward to, but it is still a very new industry, which warrants an even extra bit of caution. However, if you do your due diligence the potential for becoming one of the world's new financial leaders is within the grasp of everyone.

Thank for making it through to the end of this book, let's hope it was informative and able to provide you with all of the tools you need to achieve your goals whatever they may be.

Finally, if you found this book useful in any way, a review on Amazon is always appreciated!

Happy Investing!

Cryptocurrency

─ ─ ─ ─ ─ ❧❦❧❦ ─ ─ ─ ─ ─

*How to Make Money with Ethereum –
The Investor's Guide to Ethereum
Mining, Ethereum Trading, Blockchain,
and Smart Contracts*

by

David Blake

Table of Contents

Introduction

Cryptocurrency has been growing rapidly, and multitude businesses, entrepreneurs, and individuals have been using digital currency for different transactions. The usage of cryptocurrency offers a plethora of benefits. In fact, many people are investing in this digital money.

The following chapters will discuss what you need to know about the cryptocurrency *Ether*. Ethereum is not much different with Bitcoin. In fact, it was inspired by Bitcoin. But Ethereum managed to be better – it offers things that Bitcoin does not because Ethereum is constantly changing to meet the needs of the users that are on the network.

This book focuses on Ethereum and how you will be able to make money with Ethereum. The remarkable thing about Ethereum is that, unlike the stock market, you can invest in it without the need of having a lot of money. Once you have obtained Ether, you will be at the point where you need to decide what to do with your Ether. You can take it and invest in acquiring more Ether. Or, you can cash it out through an exchange so that you can get fiat currency.

Also in this book, you will learn some problems that you may run into when you are working with Ethereum as well as how you can write your own code with Ethereum. It is not going to be easy if you do not have any coding experience, but you will be able to do it as long as you are patient and take your time.

Chapter One:

Ethereum – What Is It?

Ethereum is a blockchain application that is decentralized, public, and programmable. While you are using Ethereum, you will be using a peer to peer contract that will make it to where you can mine and trade Ether. A Russian Canadian engineer proposed his idea for Ethereum in the year of 2013. Vitalik Buterin took what he had learned from working with Bitcoin and decided that he was going to create a blockchain application that would surpass Bitcoin. In 2014, Ethereum was funded and started the development process.

When the developers were working on Ethereum, they decided that they wanted to go beyond the peer-to-peer system and provide more services to the users that Bitcoin was not able to offer. But, as Ethereum was being developed, people began to question its security and its scalability. Even now, people are continually questioning the security and scalability of Ethereum.

In the summer of 2015 Ethereum's blockchain went live. In the beginning, Ethereum's programs were being developed by the Ethereum foundation and the Ethereum Switzerland GmbH. In the spring of 2016, the Ether token was created and held a net worth of one billion dollars. The Vox website reported, "Ethereum is a new digital currency and is a challenge to Bitcoin because of the wide range of services that Bitcoin was unable to offer."

Just like everything else, there are pros and cons of using Ethereum. In this section, you will learn these pros and cons so that you are better informed to ensure that you are making the proper decisions when it comes to investing in the future.

1. Any smart contract that is written will be executed as is.

   You most likely know whenever a contract is written by a lawyer, judges have to enforce them. But, this is an expensive process for everyone involved. That is why Ethereum offers smart contracts! Smart contracts, as you will learn later in this book, are a cheaper contract solution and are governed by the distributed autonomous organization known as the DAO.

Thanks to the distributed autonomous organization, you do not need to worry about your contract being executed any other way except how you have it written. This happens because the contracts on Ethereum have to work inside of the DAO's rules so that both parties involved in the contract are protected.

Since there is a DAO, there is no need to have judges or lawyers involved in the contract process. However, it is highly recommended that you reread your contract before you send it to the system because you are not going to be able to correct any mistakes that you make once it is in the blockchain.

2. The Distributed Autonomous Organization (DAO)

The Digix was funded by five million Ether coins so that a gold-backed cryptocurrency called Dapp could be created. All of the funding that was needed to develop Dapp was raised in a single day! Because the funding was there, the Digix Company was able to start right away without there having to be a waiting period. After the business was launched, a board was initiated to determine all of the essential aspects of the company. Some of the things that needed to be decided were how tokens would be distributed and how maintenance on the system was going to occur. Because of the board, investors, banks, and lawyers were removed from the equation; which took the stress off of investors.

The DAO took the options that were offered for contracts and placed them in a single layer so that they were simplified which allowed developers and users to be able to work on the platform in a more efficient way.

3. Fewer costs

Since Ethereum works off of the DAO, the costs that are tied to business functions are lowered because they are completed automatically. EtherEx provides a decentralized system that has a trustless cryptocurrency. EtherEx works on an infrastructure that is similar to Digix because there is a group of people that are making the crucial decisions. The foundation and the board will assist in keeping the cost of gas low for nonprofit organizations.

Whenever you look at it, a business that is built on a DAO will reduce the cost of setting up a building. You are not going to need to have your own office for your employees to use. There is still going to be a small cost that is associated with a DAO, but it is not going to be nearly as much as the businesses that are needing office supplies and buildings. On top of it, you will have the option of having an unlimited number of employees working for you.

Disadvantages

1. New

The worst thing about Ethereum is that it is still new. Therefore, it is still being developed so that the developers can create a system that will be able to offer everything that they want to be offered. But, whenever you compare Ethereum to Bitcoin, you will notice that Bitcoin is a more established system, but it is not able to provide everything that Ethereum can provide.

2. Legal

Ethereum has gotten to the point where they can get rid of the need for lawyers and judges to be involved in contracts. This will help when it comes to saving companies money, but, you will need to understand how the system works so that you are informed of the decisions that are being made on your behalf. The most significant thing that you will need to be aware of is that computers have flaws. So, a human is always going to need to be there to make sure that the computer is running as it is supposed to.

3. Changes

With the system still being new, there are always going to change that you will see coming to the platform. The system will have to shut down to apply these changes, and this can cause the servers to shut down without warning. This will be bad if you are working on a deadline and are not able to get on the network and complete your work on time.

Chapter One: Ethereum – What Is It?

Throughout the rest of this book, you will see how you will be able to make money with Ethereum. But, it is always an excellent idea to know the pros and cons of the network that you are working with.

Chapter Two:

Ethereum's Blockchain

Ethereum's blockchain is just like the blockchain that you see when you are using Bitcoin. The chain contains a ledger that holds every transaction that is completed on the system so that users can see what has been done and who has done it.

On top of that, it uses an encryption service known as cryptography so that the data that is in the chain is not getting out to someone that does not need access to it. The encryption protects the coins that are used on the blockchain so that they cannot be counterfeited or hacked as well.

Ethereum's blockchain is created based on what is recorded on the block that comes before it. Each block will be built when transactions are verified and accepted into the chain.

Cryptocurrency

The blockchain is completely secured which means that it cannot be hacked. So, any transactions that are completed are not going to be tampered with at all. That is excellent news for those that use the blockchain because they do not have to worry about someone messing with the work that they do to get their rewards.

Chapter Three:

The Possible Problems You May Face with Ethereum

Ethereum has been evolving. And as it grows, the system improves. Hence, we can expect that there are still some downsides and flaws while it is still in the development process. These problems may stop the users from controlling the platform freely. But understanding the issues will help you big time. It will help you avoid the issues, thus allowing you to continue to use the system smoothly.

One of the problems that you may run into with ethereum is its scalability. In an article, Economist and Investor Tuur Demeester said: "I'm not worried about Bitcoin scalability, but I am losing sleep over Ethereum." The scalability of Ethereum is weak, and it is because the design of the blockchain relies on bottleneck where every single transaction in the entire network is being processed by individual nodes.

Here are some of the problems that cause an issue in the scalability of Ethereum:

- The number of users that are on the network

- The usage of specialized and unspecialized hardware. Specialized hardware is more powerful than unspecialized hardware. Apparently, the majority of users use unspecialized equipment.

Another problem that you may face with Ethereum is the time stamping. Basically, a block is created every ten minutes. However, when a block is being built every day, that will mean that the system will go slow. Also, if the blocks are constructed too fast, the platform will be overwhelmed, thus causing issues in the performance of the platform.

If you face any of these issues, you need to report it to the developers. These geeks will try their best to fix the problem so that it will not affect other users. Developers are human too. They make mistakes. But, rest assured, just as how we try to improve our ways, we can expect them doing the same. Hence, if you are having problems with ethereum, no matter how small or big the issue is, you must coordinate with the developers.

There will be issues that will come up from time to time. You can help improve the platform of Ethereum if you inform the developers about it. You can also seek help from other users. They may have faced the problem you are having, and they may have solved that.

Chapter Four:

How to Make Money with Ethereum

E thereum is a platform where you can make money in both Ether and fiat currency. Some of the ways that you will see in this chapter are also going to be explained later on in the book. Here are ideas of how you can make money with Ethereum:

Buy and sell

At this point in time, Ethereum is like to Bitcoin when it was first started in 2009. Buying Ether could make you money because the price will go up and if you are able to catch the price at the right time, then you will be able to sell it at twice the amount that you first bought it at.

Cryptocurrency

Here are a few reasons that you will want to consider purchasing Ether for long-term investments.

    a. The technology that is under Ethereum will be able to be used for a number of purposes since it is an autonomous and decentralized system. In other words, there is a broad range of industries that will be able to use Ethereum.

    b. The demand for the Ethereum platform continues to increase which means that the price of Ether will surge.

    c. The developers behind Ethereum have created a system that works off of a giant computer allowing applications to run at the same time thus allowing people to be able to do multiple things on the Ethereum blockchain at the same time.

    d. For the most part, Ethereum has shown growth without any spikes which cause it to be predictable and even stable. As the demand for Ethereum increases, the value of the Ether token will increase

e. Ethereum is making waves in industries
    that are already established such as
    Microsoft. Microsoft offers a blockchain
    service that its users will be able to use
    with their games.

Using Coinbase

Step one: go to coin base and sign up for a coin base account. With this account, you will have somewhere that you can store your Ether and make payments so that you can convert your currency into Ether or your Ether into money.

Step two: insert your payment method of choice. It can be a credit card or your bank account.

Step three: Choose the buy/sell button

Step four: select the amount of Ether that you want to purchase.

Step five: click on buy Ethereum.

Note: Coin base has a fee of 1.49 – 3.99% depending on what your payment method is. Credit cards are usually going to have a higher price than a wire transfer have.

Cryptocurrency

Using Cex.io

Step one: you will need to open a Cex.io account

Step two: insert your payment method of choice.

Step three: you will then go to the buy/sell option before you select Ethereum.

Step four: pick how much Ether you want to buy or sell

Step five: select the final button to finish out your transaction.

Mining

To mine, you will need to know your way around a computer. Once you have mined Ether, you will want to hold onto it while you watch the value of Ether go up before you sell it to someone else. To mine on Ethereum, you will have to get specific pieces of software and programs to mine correctly. But, you will see more about that in chapter five.

Investing

Usually, this is an obvious option. However, you are still going to want to have the steps to invest on Ethereum properly. Please keep in mind that you will need to do your research so that you are investing correctly and making money rather than wasting it.

Step one: research the companies that are using Ethereum

Step two: select the amount of Ether or money that you want to invest in that company

Step three: watch the stocks of the company and cash out whenever that company's shares are high, and you can make a profit.

Chapter Five:

Trading Ethereum

Once you have obtained some Ether, you will be able to transfer them to an exchange so that you can begin trading. The process for moving your cryptocurrency to an exchange will vary depending on the exchange that you are using. For example, if you are using Poloniex you are no longer going to be able to register and make trades if you are living in New York. This policy was put in place because of various regulations that Poloniex thinks are too expensive to deal with.

Therefore, once you have gotten Ether, you will want to use Kraken. Kraken is one of the highest ranked exchanges and has a good reputation, not to mention it is one of the first exchanges that started trading Ether.

Cryptocurrency

The first step will be to open an account. Opening an account will be similar to any other site that you have opened an account on, you will use your email and create a password to get into the account.

Next, you will need to go through all of their compliance steps which are typical steps that will be taken in verifying your address. There are various levels of registration depending on the information that is provided by you. The first two levels will be the levels that allow you to trade and pull out a decent amount of cryptocurrency; and, all you will need to input is your address and your phone number. However, if you want to trade on a larger scale, you will be required to register your passport and a utility bill to prove your address.

After you have gotten through all the levels of verification so that you can complete trades, then you will deposit Ether or fiat currency. Thankfully Kraken provides instructions on how to deposit money into your account. Making any sort of deposit will generate an address that your funds will be sent from.

You will then need to create a transaction. After that has been done, Ethereum will appear in your account after a short amount of time.

Once your transaction has been confirmed and the sufficient amount of time has passed, you will be allowed to start trading. To work out the best price, you will want to use a combination of the trading platforms to look at prices across the board to ensure that you are not paying a higher fee than someone else would on a different website.

Chapter Six:

Mining Ethereum

Mining Ethereum means that you will be solving algorithms to receive a reward. In this section of the book, you will learn what is required to mine Ether.

Step one: Download Geth.

You will need to download Geth onto your computer. This is the program that will communicate with Ethereum and be the relay point between your computer and the network. Therefore, if a block is mined by a different computer, your computer will pick up on that and move the information to your GPU for mining.

Step two: Unzip Geth.

Unzip the file that Geth comes in so that it can be placed on your hard drive. You will right click on the file that is zipped and pick the unpack button. When this happens, you will move it to your hard drive (usually the C drive) to make the next step easier. To move it to the hard drive, you will copy the downloaded file and past it into your hard drive folder.

Step three: start the command prompt.

From here you have to run the program that you just placed on your hard drive. To do this, you will run the command prompt. This can be done by searching in the search function on your computer for CMD and then clicking on it once it appears on your screen.

Step four: cd into the root directory.

The command prompt will be open after you searched CMD in the last step. Most of the time the command prompt scares people because they are not familiar with it. But, the command prompt is typically going to look like this.

C:\Users\Username>

The username is obviously going to be your username that you log into your computer with when you are using it. The next thing that you will see is the crypto compare command prompt box. This can be opened by inserting the following code.

C:\Users\cryptocompare

You will need to inform your computer to search another location on your hard drive. In the new command prompt, you will type.

Cd /

It is then going to be changed to

C: \ >

You have successfully used a cd command (change directory) to force the command prompt to search your C hard drive.

Step five: make your Geth account

The Geth program needs to be told that a new account has to be made. Once it has been installed in your user directory, you will use the command prompt again and enter

Geth account new

Cryptocurrency

Once you have sent that to the network, you will get this response

Geth account new

Step six: create your password.

After the enter button is hit in the previous step, you are not going to see what is being typed. Therefore, you must type carefully. The password you create will lock your account and protect your currency as well as your private key.

Note: If you lose the password, then all of your Ether and your private key will be lost for good!

After the password has been entered, you will confirm it one more time before a new account is created.

Step seven: connect to Ethereum.

Still using Geth, you will need to tell it to communicate with the rest of the Ethereum network. To do this, you will enter

Geth --rpc

Geth should change it so that it looks like this

C:\> Geth --rpc

You will now press the enter button, and on your screen, you should see the blockchain downloading. During this process, you will be downloading the rest of the Ethereum network that you will need to work. Your firewall may block the process, but you need to allow access.

Step eight: download the mining software.

Here, you will need to install Ethminer. This program will take your GPU or CPU and run it as a hashing algorithm that will be vital in securing the network for Ethereum for proof of work. Make sure that you are scrolling all the way to the bottom of the page to get the correct version.

Step nine: install your mining software.

You need to click on the file that you have downloaded and choose the install option. There is the possibility that your firewall will cause some issues. If this is the case, then you will click on the "allow" button so that your internet connection is no longer blocked. The same thing will happen in the event that your computer does not recognize the software. You will need to let Windows know that it is okay for the software to be placed on your machine. Once you have done that, you will need to go through the installation process with Ethminer.

Step ten: start your command prompt again.

You will open the command prompt like you did in step four. Now, you will right-click on your command prompt that appears in the taskbar at the bottom and select the command prompt that appears in the menu. Another command prompt should open showing you the same code that you saw when you first opened the command prompt. But, this is the wrong place to locate Ether miner.

Step eleven: locate your Ether miner directory in your new command prompt

Insert:

Cd /

It should change to look something like this.

C: \ users\ username >cd /

Once you hit enter, it will change again to look like this

C: / >

Step twelve: change cd into the program files.

You need to enter

Cd prog.

After you have done that, you should hit tab so that the code changes to

C:/ > cd prog

Hitting tab again will complete your phrase to the closest fit that can be found on the c drive. It will be similar to using auto-complete on your phone.

Now that you have hit tab again you should see something like this.

C:/ > cd "program files"

Hit enter so that you receive a new line that says

C:/ program files >

Cryptocurrency

Step thirteen: cd into your Ethereum folder

Enter

Cd eth

Here is when you will hit tab and then enter so that you are taken to the Ethereum mining software folder. After you puh tab once more, your command prompt code should change to look something like this.

C:\Program Files>cd "Ethereum (++) 0.9.39

Note: your code may look a little different if you are using a different version.

Step fourteen: cd into the release folder.

The first thing that you will do is enter

Cd release

Upon hitting enter, you will get a new line that says.

C:\Program   Files\Ethereum   (++)
0.9.39\Release>

Step fifteen: GPU mining

Enter:

ethminer -G

You need to hit enter so that you can begin mining with your GPU (this is the best way to mine). Once you have completed the DAG file, then you can mine. Building the DAG file will take around ten minutes.

One problem that you may run into is that you do not have the proper amount of memory. If you run into this problem, then you can still mine, but you will need to use your CPU or go and purchase another graphics card. In the event that you get the message, you will want to hit control and C so that you can cancel the process. From there you can retry or move on to the next step so that you can continue to mine Ether.

Step sixteen: CPU mining

In your command prompt, enter

Ethminer

Once you hit enter, you will be able to use your CPU to mine Ether. You are still going to need to create a DAG file the first time that you do any mining. But, once it has been built, the Geth program that you already downloaded will start communicating with the Etherminer program and begin mining.

Chapter Seven:

How to Buy Ethereum

You saw some ways that you can buy and sell Ether in a previous chapter. But, let's get into it more so that you have a better understanding of what you are doing.

The first thing you need to be aware of is that there are scams and phishing sites that will mimic real sites so that they can take your money. You need to make sure you are verifying the sites you want to use.

Another thing is to make sure you are keeping your private key backed up in a separate location. Try to avoid using cloud storage since those can be hacked.

The last thing to keep in mind is that you need to be skeptical. If it seems too good to be true, then it probably is.

Cryptocurrency

Now, here is how you will buy Ether.

Step one: you need an account on websites like Coin base, Kraken, or Gemini.

Step two: verify your account. Each site will have its own set of requirements when it comes to proving your identity. Sometimes the verification process will take a day or two depending on how busy the service is. Just be patient because your information will be verified as soon as possible.

Step three: there will be instructions that you have to follow to deposit money. Depending on the communication that your bank has set up, it could take up to five days for the funds to appear in your account.

Step four: once you have money in your account, you will be able to use it to purchase Ether.

Step five: after you have purchased the amount of Ether that you want, you will be able to pull that currency out and put it into a wallet that only you have access to. It is recommended that you do this as soon as you make your purchase because exchanges are easy for people to hack into and you are not going to want to have your funds in an area that someone else will be able to access.

Step six: as you are waiting for your verification or transfers to go through, you will need to install Mist and the Ethereum Wallet so that they can sync to the blockchain.

Step seven: while you're running the blockchain it will ask you to create a new account. You will need to create a password that you are not going to forget easily. Once your account is created, an address will be assigned to you and it will start with ox. The address will be what you enter when you want to pull your Ether off the exchange and put it into your own account.

Step eight: Keep these three pieces of information safe so that no one can get into your account.

    a. Your private key

    b. Your address

    c. Your password

Cryptocurrency

Alternate steps for 1-5

In the event that you already have Bitcoin, then you will be able to use Shapeshift.io to convert it over to Ether. You will start a BTC to ETC exchange, and then you will be told where you should send your BTC. Should your BTC already be on an exchange, you may be able to complete your exchange without shapeshifting.

After that, you need to have an Ethereum wallet and keep it backed up. Coin base and Circle allow you to send your BTC to a specific address and your Ether will appear in the wallet within twenty minutes.

Alternatives steps for 6-8

The Ethereum wallet is one of the most recommended wallets; but, there are some who find that they have issues installing and syncing it on their computer. If you find that you have this problem, you will be able to find different wallets to use.

Chapter Eight:

Smart Contracts

The blockchain that Bitcoin and Ethereum use was created when Bitcoin was established in 2009. But, when Ethereum was developed, a new piece of technology was designed to keep up with the changes that were being made in the cryptocurrency world; this new piece of technology was called smart contracts. In this chapter, you will learn how to create your smart contract as well as how to analyze it. This will come in handy when you are looking over your contract before you send it to the blockchain network to ensure that you did not leave anything out.

Terms to remember

1. Public key cryptography: your public key will be a two-part system. Not only will your public key be public, but it will be

your virtual signature that will be placed on all of your blockchain transactions. It is crucial that you back up your key so that you can continue to have access to your accounts since there is no way for you to access the key externally in the event that you lose it.

2. Ethereum virtual machine: the location in which smart contracts are written out in the blockchain infrastructure that is appropriate for the contract at hand. (You will learn more about the virtual machine in a later chapter).

3. dApp: a decentralized application that is used with smart contracts so that they can be placed on the Ethereum marketplace. dApp runs from a central location or from Ethereum nodes.

4. Blockchain: the public ledger that contains every transaction done on a cryptocurrency network.

5. Ether: Ethereum's value token. Ether is commonly referred to as ETH. One ETH is worth sixty-five cents in USD.

Creating your contract

You do not have to have your own Ethereum node when you are designing your contract, but it is recommended because it makes deploying your contract easier. When you use the node, you will have the power to connect to the Ethereum network as a whole; this includes having access to Java, Python, Haskell, and C++.

Solidity tool is the programming language that you will be using when you create your contract. Essentially, Solidity is the JavaScript for Ethereum and will end in the extension of .sol or .se.

It is vital that you are using a compiler! You should also make sure that you have the C++ library so that you can ensure that you have all of the tools that you need to write your contract. When you download C++, you will not be required to download Solc.

If you do not want to download C++ then you can use the web version which will be located on Etherechain.org; you can also use Cosmo. One of the last things that you will need to do is download web3.ja; it is an API application that will be used when creating dApp.

Cryptocurrency

At the point in time that your Solidity contract is compiled, it will be sent back to the network. From there, your contract will be recalled by using web3.js. This is the moment that you will have the option of building a web application to interact with your contract accordingly.

In the event that you are interested in taking advantage of the existing framework, then you will be using a distributed application known as Truffle. Truffle is the most recommended by developers when it comes to using a program that is easy to understand while allowing for a significant emphasis to be placed on specific code. If you do not own a node, then you will be using blockapps.net. Blockapps.net is an API that will allow you to use a node for testing purposes without actually having your own node.

Some contracts have specifics that will vary based on the variables placed in the contract. For example, if an event occurs then there will be a result that is kept in a log to show that the agreement was met as it was supposed to be. This will not affect how the deal acts; but, at the same time, there is a function that will alter the yes and no state that is in the contract by modifying the values that are in place before the contract is activated. This happens because the function moves from one account to another whenever the conditions are met.

A contract's address will be able to locate where your wallet is and if the contract has access to the wallet through its unique address. This will be a separate address from your wallet's address. The next variable you need to worry about is how big your contract is; the smaller the contract is, then the better it will run on the network. The smart contracts will have the ability to pull data from the Ethereum oracle through a public variable that will determine if the data has to be consulted or not as well as where the information is coming from.

Think about this

While writing out your smart contract, you have to look at the information that you are working with so that you can store all of the data in the contract for the terms to be met. You need to have a list of items that will determine the overall structure of the file that you are working with. Usually, this data will be stored in a 2-xn mapping sequence. N will be how many transactions need to be finished along with the details that will go with that transaction.

You should keep in mind what outcome you are working towards because you will need to include the definition of two struts. Your first strut will consist of information for the user that started the transaction ; this means that the number of transactions that will be involved in that strut.

The second strut will contain the data for the storage of information that needs to be included for the mapping that will occur in the contract so it is laid out as it should be. This strut is primarily going to be the outline of the database that you are working with; it will automatically label the contracts based on your template.

Afer you are done with the template creation, you will need to define your functions that need to be executed on a regular basis along with any prompts that will be required to complete the transaction. All of the proper transactions will be sent to the owner of the contract. This idea was first proposed so that it could include the limits of the transactions that are added, any stipulations that are placed on the contract, and the funds in the contract's account.

An investor's transaction will include a unique ID that will be stored in the space that is set aside for the record that will be linked to the contract. This area will be set aside beforehand by the system for all of the contract's outcomes so that they are in the same place and can be found again at a later date. Should there be a time limit on the transaction, then a final deal will be generated. This agreement will trigger the last action which is usually referred to as a suicide action to stop the contract from being rerun.

Here is where the user will have the opportunity to decide what they want to do with the funds that they have received. Their results will be tested once the contract has been uploaded to the blockchain. Dummy contracts will list you as the investor if that is how you plan on checking your contract. It will be required that you go through all of the motions of interacting with your contract to ensure that it reacts the way that you want it to.

Cryptocurrency

The execution process

Like you read about earlier, Truffle is the programming process that makes it so that your contract is more manageable in the event that you are not comfortable placing all of your information in one place before you test the code first. To assist in the writing process, Truffle will check the scenarios in the contract through the Java framework. You need to remember that your contract will take about ten seconds to be verified, and that is only going to happen if you have written out everything correctly; it will take longer if your contract is not written right. It is vital that you take the time into account when you are testing your contract's code.

You also need to have access to the window console where you are writing your smart contract that way a new node can be created once the Truffle program has been opened.

Whenever you use your deploy command, Truffle will be deployed and create a spaw in the basics of the init of your contract. Your code will be tested by compiling all of the scripts and checking it for any errors that may have occurred.

The next step

After the contract has been written, it will need to be formatted to be placed on the blockchain; and you will do this by using Solidity's online formatter which will be located at Etherchain.org/solc. During this step, your code will be formatted, and you will then be allowed to upload the contract by paying a small portion of Ether so that you can get a signature box. In this signature box, you will need to place your private key so that you can make the contract yours. You will then receive the results through an ABI and the blockchain address where all of the data will be stored for the remainder of the contracts life.

Now that you have compiled your contract and deployed it by using Truffle, you will need to open the Truffle console and go to the new directory by using the init command. A new index will be created, and it will add the .sol extension to your contract. From there you will need to enter config/app.sol so that you can add your contract to the space that has been set aside for it. Once all that has been completed, you will have to restart your program before running the tesrpc command. By doing this, Truffle will be deployed at the root level; however, your contract will be live on the Ethereum blockchain.

There will be a user interface that will be formed after you have created your contract, and this will be where you interact with your contract in real time. The dApp will be placed inside of the database that consists of an HTML based front end and will be tied into the Ethereum platform. Should you be using Truffle, then the dApp will connect it to a complete network as long as there is CDN access. The dApp UI will be designed in such a way that it will be similar to how a website is designed.

You will notice that there are various frameworks in place to help you with your dApp creation so that it is easier for you to manage. Just like you saw above, Truffle is a tool that you can use, but it is not the only one out there. You also have the option of using Embark; however, Truffle will be the most straightforward tool that you will have the option of using.

As you use Truffle, you will be creating your smart contract. But, you should know that there will be other things that you can use Truffle for, and you need to have all of the information so that you can make an informed decision as to what is the best application for you.

Truffle will complete most of the work for you when it comes to working with smart contracts and dApps.

Embark applications will help in deploying contracts so that they are available in the JS code of your choice. Embark will make it so that changes are tracked so you can see where your contract has been updated. If this happens, then Embark will redeploy your contract automatically.

Creating dApp

Whenever a dApp is created, you will want to use Truffle because it will compile your UI after it has been established automatically. Truffle's director will need to be labeled so that the next time that it is run, it will compile all of the contact information; it will also collect new changes into the build folder so that the program can call upon it in case an emergency occurs with the Truffle application.

In order to use the directory, it needs to be labeled as an application so that it has the chance to find background images and use the JavaScript code that is connected to the indexes and stylesheets in the directory. Depending on what is needed, you will have the option of inserting code directly into the file that is already there so that you can use the front end UI option to get your contract up faster. Once you open the app.js file, then you will see a section that will give you a greeting from Truffle in your developer console. Once you open this console, then you will see a list of active commands.

When you are looking at the commands, you will notice that you need to create a function that can be accessed whenever a page is loaded. To do this, you need a window that will be added by using a code window when loading the app.js file. If you can do this right, then you will have an assortment of details about your account that will be shown in the console's browser. The last thing that you need to do is test the conference.js function to make sure that your output is working the way that it needs to be working. Your output has to be an equal amount, and the balance will increase once a situation is deferred.

At the point in time that the app.js is created with the index.html, then it will be able to meet all of the needs that are required to test the results from your node so that you end up receiving results in real time.

Tip: your results are not going to be prepared quickly. You will need to use the following code to make sure that it is working the way that it is supposed to.

```
Geth--rpc --rpcaddr="0.0.0.0"--
rpccorsdomain="*"--mine --unlock='0
1'verbosity=5--maxpeers=0--minerthreads='4'--
networkid '12345'--genesis testgenesis. json
```

There will now be two new accounts that will be labeled zero and one. The thing to remember is that each account will have a password that will be generated along with a json test-genesis file; you can find this file under the alloc tab on your account which is also going to be where your Ether costs will be kept. You will also need to add the results to your Truffle application to recompile the contract and deploy your results again.

There is an option that you can use to generate the UI which you can use with any dApp that has been created with the silent ciero. This application can be found at dappbuilder.metor.com. It is this tool that you will use when you are writing HTML code so that it can be modified later when you are finishing your contract in Solidity, web3.js, or jQuery. But, this application is not going to run as smoothly as you will want it to if you are not comfortable with your skill level. UI will follow the same steps as the ones that have already been laid out in this chapter. If it does not, then there will be another version that will most likely be easier for you to use when you are trying to find a solution to the issue that you are having.

At this point in the process, the contract should be written entirely, but you will not be done with it just yet. You need to analyze your contract. As you examine it, you need o ensure that it has been written correctly and that you fix anything that needs to be fixed.

Let's examine the variables that you will see at the top of your smart contract.

Address public organizer;

Mapping (address => uint) public registrants Paid;

Uint public nonresistant;

Uint public quota;

Address: being that this is the first variable in your contract, it will be the address for your wallet. The address needs to be set whenever the constructor is so that a conference is created. However, in most cases, the contract will name it the owner.

Unit: the unit will be an unsigned integer. You will have a space on the blockchain for your contract, but it is not going to be very large, which is why you need to attempt to try and keep everything as small as you can.

Public: the public variable will be called from the outside of the contract that you complete. When it comes to working with a private modifier, the contract will call upon it. But, when you try and call on the variable from web3.js, the variable has to be public.

Mapping an array: there are various levels of support for the arrays and mapping in your smart contract. For example address = > unit that will be used by Solidity. The mapping will contain a smaller footprint. So, your mapping

Cryptocurrency

will be used to store the registrant that paid for it so that the funds are available at a later date.

Extra address: a client node will hold your account data. When you start your tests, there will be around ten addresses available for you to use. The zero account will be the default account when a state is not specified for the transaction.

Organizer address and contract addresses: each contract will have its own address after it has been deployed. The contract address will be different than the organizer address. The organizer address will be located through the Solidity contract. You will use it for the refund ticket function.

Suicide and Solidity: if funds are sent to your contract, then the contract will hold on to them until the contract's obligations are fulfilled. By using the destroy function, you will have the resources released to the owner of the contract. If this is not put in place, the funds will be tied up, and no one will have access to them. Therefore, it is crucial that you include a suicide method in each contract that you write just in case your contract dies, that way you can collect the funds.

But, if you are simulating another party in the contract, you will have the option of inserting another address that will be different from the accounts that are in the array. For example, if you want to buy a ticket to the dance you will need to purchase it with this function.

Conference. buy Ticket ({

      From: accounts [1], value: some_ticket_price_integer});

Function calls that are transactions: a function has the ability to change the state of your contract, and these deals will include a specific sender and value that will be located in a set of curly braces. Any funds that are available will be transferred to the wallet's address. With Solidity, you will be allowed to retrieve values with the msg sender and ms value function.

Function buy Ticket () public {

    ...

registrants Paid [msg. sender] = msg. value;

    ...

    }

Cryptocurrency

Events: an event will be an option when you are writing your contract. Deposits can be set up to be sent in the contract, but they also need to be logged with the virtual machine. However, they are not going to do anything; it is merely good practice so that you can keep track of everything that has happened with your transaction already.

Chapter Nine:

Ethereum's Virtual Machine

E thereum's virtual machine will focus on providing security as well as carrying out untrusted computer code. More specifically, it will work to prevent denial of service attacks (DOS). Attacks like this have become more common amongst cryptocurrency networks. But, the Ethereum virtual machine will make sure that programs do not get access to another program's state all while making sure that there is an open line of communication without interference.

Now, that probably went over your head, so let's look at it in a way that will make a little more sense to you.

The Ethereum virtual machine will serve as a runtime environment for any smart contract that is on the Ethereum network. For most enthusiasts of cryptocurrency, they know that smart contracts continue to grow in popularity. The Ethereum blockchain technology can be used so that transactions are automatically conducted; it can also perform specific actions that need to completed on the blockchain. There are a lot of people who are beginning to realize that smart contracts will revolutionize the financial industry and several other sectors as it develops more.

It has even speculated that the Ethereum virtual machine was written about in Dr. Gavin Wood'sYellow Paper. You can look at the Ethereum project and realize that it was built with the perspective of introducing a sandbox environment so that smart contract technology could be honed in more thus making them better in the future.

All it takes is a single piece of code to help elevate Ethereum and smart contracts to the next level, and Ethereum developers are continually working to find that piece of code!

Being that the Ethereum virtual machine is isolated from the rest of the Ethereum network, it is the perfect environment to test code. Whenever a company wants to write a smart contract, the virtual machine can be used without affecting the primary blockchain operation. Doing the tests is vital, but you can also look at the virtual machine as a learning environment where you can build better smart contracts.

Each Ethereum node will have its own EVM implementation and can execute the same instructions that are placed in the EVM. It is evident that the EVM has a bright future as it continues to update. But, in the end, the EVM is going will be the gateway that you use to build a proper contract; even if you are an experienced code. The EVM has been implemented in various coding languages like Python, C++, and Ruby.

While a sandbox environment is not necessarily a bad thing, it is still in its early stages, so it is continually changing the system. The Ethereum virtual machine had decentralized a wide range of day to day operations for big industries with the help of smart contracts.

It is recommended that if you use cryptocurrency, you keep an eye on the new developments that come through with the EVM and smart contracts because, in the end, this technology will change the world of cryptocurrency!

Chapter Ten:

The Ethereum Enterprise Alliance

A lot of global companies have taken an interest in Ethereum because the blockchain foundation offers a lot of technological innovations. One innovation has been smart contracts; these smart contracts have added a lot of value to enterprises and started ups across the world. Most of the companies that have taken advantage of the technology have been those that are on the fortune 500 lists as well as those that are in the financial sector.

And this is why the Ethereum enterprise alliance was formed! There has been a lot of progress when it comes to smart contract technology as you have seen, and because of this, it has made Ethereum the leading smart contract blockchain when it comes to real-world production.

Cryptocurrency

When you look at the enterprise blockchain's point of view, the Ethereum blockchain will make more sense. This technology has not only been tested in a sandbox environment, but it has been tested by users in a wide range of projects over the years. The multiple purpose design has aided in furthering research by technology enthusiasts, enterprises, and those in academics. To top it off, every project that is built by an enterprise alliance member is open sourced and ready to be used by everyone on the Ethereum blockchain.

The Ethereum enterprise alliance is not trying to create a product. Instead, they want to develop an industry-wide standard for all that participate. Moreover, every team is trying to address the deployment requirements that each enterprise has. Because of this, the Ethereum enterprise alliance is trying to make it so that Ethereum responds to every need that these companies have so that they stay on the Ethereum blockchain instead of trying to find another platform that will give them what they want.

It will be interesting to watch the Ethereum enterprise alliance evolve along with the public

Chapter Ten: The Ethereum Enterprise Alliance

Ethereum network. There is still going to be leveraging existing standards, but there are also going to be a lot of new improvements that members will start to see as well. The enterprise alliance team is beginning going to reveal their roadmap for the features that the enterprise will have in the next few months along with identifying how an industry plans to specifically use Ethereum for the network to develop around those needs.

There are a lot of prominent members that are already a part of the Ethereum enterprise alliance such as Microsoft, Consensys, BBVA, BNY Mellon, and Credit Suisse. There are plenty of other industries that are in the EEA. However, their names may not be released yet because they do not know if the EEA will benefit them or not.

In the end, the Ethereum Enterprise Alliance was created to try and help big industries and start-up companies choose Ethereum over other blockchains that are out there. They want these companies to bring their money to Ethereum so that it can be used to better the network rather than see it be used somewhere else. The Ethereum enterprise alliance is trying to make it to where these companies can use Ethereum in

Cryptocurrency

the manner that they want to use it rather than having to worry that they will need to compromise and possibly miss out on business opportunities that they are working towards.

And, while the Ethereum enterprise alliance creates a better Ethereum for industries, it ends up building a better Ethereum network for everyone.

Chapter Eleven:

Programming with Ethereum

When you are programming with Ethereum, there will be a couple of different languages that can be used. In the event that you are familiar with Java or C then you will find that Solidity is similar and will be easy for you to understand. However, if you enjoy using Lisp or other functional languages, you may discover that LLL will be the programming language that you use most often. But, the mutant language will be similar to C, and in this chapter, you will see Serpent 2.0. The serpent will be identical to Python; and even if you are not familiar with Python, you can quickly pick up Serpent.

Note: if you test the code that you see in this section, you will need to use the serpent_code

Cryptocurrency

variable. Also, a lot of the built-in functions from Serpent 1.0 will work for Serpent 2.0.

Log () function

When you use the log function, it will be easy for you to run a debugging process. Should your X be defined as a variable, then you will need to find the output. To do this, you will use log (x) which will give you the output for the contents of the variable.

Example

Def main (n) :

Log (n)

Return (n)

The code will produce an output that will be stored in the n variable. If you were to pass it in a three, then it would be stored in a three.

Example:

('Log' ,
'c305c901078781c232a2a521c2af7980f8385ee9'
, [3L] , [ ])

Chapter Eleven: Programming with Ethereum

The most important part of the code will be the third piece of data that you will find stored in a tuple, more specifically, [3L]. That is where you see that the value of the variable is three.

Variables

If you want to assign a variable to Serpent, it will be a relatively simple process. All you need to do is set the variable equal to what you want the variable to be equal to.

Example

D = 345

U = z

Special variables

There are a few special variables that you will be able to use with Serpent. Each of these unique variables will reference specific pieces of data or parts of the blockchain that is important to your code. Below you will see these special variables and what they will be used for.

Tx. Origin: the address where the address for the transaction is sent from.

Cryptocurrency

Tx. Gas prices: the cost of gas in the most current transaction will be stored here.

Tx. Gas: the gas that remains will be placed in this transaction.

Msg. Sender: the address of the person that is sending out information to be processed into the contract will be placed here.

Msg. Value: the amount of Ether that is sent with the message will be measured in Wei.

Self: the address of the contract

Self. Balance: how much Ether the contract controls

x. balance: the x will be an address, and the balance is how much Ether is in that account.

Block coin base: the address of a miner will be stored.

Block. Timestamp: the current timestamp will be stored

Block. Prevhash: the hash that occurred on the previous block will be stored.

Block. Difficulty: the difficulty from the current block will be stored.

Block. Number: the numeric identifier for the current block will be stored.

Block. Gaslimit: the gas limit for the current block will be stored.

Note: *Wei* will be the smallest unit of Ether possible. Whenever Ether is referred to in terms of wei, then it will be in terms of a contract.

Control flow

When it comes to using Serpent, you will be using if...elif...else statements that will control the programs that you use.

Example

W = 6

X = 6

Y = 6

If w == y

W = w + 6

Cryptocurrency

$Y = y - 6$

$X = 0$

Return (x)

Elif x = y :

$Y = 4$

Return (x)

Else:

Return (0)

When you are using Serpent, you will need to put tabs in, and it is important because if anything is in line with the tabbed section after the if statement, then it will think that the statement is true and run it as such. The same thing goes with the elif and the else statement. You will notice that this is also going to apply to functions and loops which you will see later on.

The not modifier

Syntax:

If not a == b:

Return (c)

The code that you just saw is not going to run unless a is equal to b. Even then, it is only going to run in the event that they are different. You will see that the not modifier is similar to the ! modifier that is in Java and a couple of other programming languages.

Loops

The serpent will support a loop as long as they are used as the following example.

Anumber = 5

While anothernumber > 4:

Log (anumber)

A number = another number − 4

The loop code will store each number starting at 5 until it reaches 4.

Array

Cryptocurrency

Example

Def main () :

Arra = array (3453)

Arra [5] = 9

Arra [879] = 32

Return (arra [879])

In the code that you see above, you will be creating an array the size of 3453 and the number 9 will be assigned to the zero-th index while 32 is attached to the 879th index. The index will return 879 because he values that is at that index.

Some functions that will be used with arrays in Serpent are:

Slice (arr, items = s, items = e): array will be the array while *s* is the address where the array starts, and e is where the address ends. You can split the function out into portions of the array that land between s and e so that s < = e is returned.

Len (arr): the length of the array will be returned.

When returning an array, you need to append :arr to the end o the array that is located on the return statement.

Example

Def main ():

Arra = array (15)

Arra [1] = 15

Arra [4] = 54

Return (arra: arr)

You should get the array returned to you where the values have been initialized to zero, and the address has also been initialized.

Strings

There are two types of strings that will be used with Serpent. The first series that will be used will be known as a short string. These strings will be treated as a number and will be able to be manipulated as such. A long series will be treated

Cryptocurrency

as an array by Serpent. You may notice that long strings are similar to the strings that are found in C. Should you be a contract programmer then you need to know what variables go with short strings and which ones go with the long strings because they need to be treated differently.

Short string

Short strings will be the easiest to work with since they are treated like numbers by Serpent.

Example

Stra = string a

Strb = string b

Strc = string c

And, it is just as simple when you want to compare to short strings.

Example

Return (stra == strb)

Return (stra == strc)

The very first statement will give you an output of a which will show that the string is valid; but, at the same time, the second string will provide you with an output of zero, and that will mean that the string is false.

Long strings

A long string will be implemented using the same process that is used in the C programming language because the string will be a list of characters. There are a couple of commands that you can use when you are working with long strings.

To define a new string you will use: arbitrary_string = text

If you want to change one character that is listed in the string, you will use: arbitrary_string= text sketch (arbitrary_string, 5, a)

The sketch () function will change the variable that is listed at the index that you put into it. So if you want to change what is in the fifth index, you will put five into the code and what you want it to be changed to. Once you deploy the script, it will make the changes that you wish to be made automatically.

Cryptocurrency

Should you want to use an ASCII value at an index, you need to use this code.

Arbitrary_string= text getch(arbitrary_string, index number)

By using this code, you will be retrieving the ASCII value at the index value for the string that you will work with.

Note: every function that you use in an array will work on a long string.

To check the equality of two strings, you may run into a few problems, but you can do it as long as you learn how to use the getch () method.

Example

Def compare_equals ():

Stra = numbers

Strb = numbers

A = 3

While a < len (stra):

If getch (stra , a) ! = getch (strb , a):

Return (-3)

A = a + a

Return (a)

Functions

A function that is placed in Ethereum will work just like every other programming language that you could be using. If you look at the previous examples, you will have some idea as to how a function will work in Ethereum.

Example:

Def main ():

#an operation

Return (0)

Now let's look at an example that contains three parameters.

Def main (a, b, c):

an operation

Return (0)

Cryptocurrency

It is recommended that you always define your functions so that your code is not only easier to read but easier to write. But, how do you call these functions out when you are working on a contract? You will use the self.function_name (params). When you reference a function that is inside of the contract, you will need to call it from the self-function.

Note: a function will be called directly by the users. So if you have a function labeled one and another function marked two should two have the logic that will send out Ether, then one will check to see if the Ether has been sent like it is supposed to be. One is also going to call two when it comes time to deliver the Ether. So, in the end, two will be a call function and cannot work without the check. You will be able to fix this issue by not placing the type of logic in a different function.

Special function block

There are at least three different unique function blocks that you can use. These blocks will be used when it comes time to declare a function which is always going to be executed before another function.

The first one is the init function. This function will be run a single time, and that will happen when the function is first created. Init will be good for when you need to declare a variable before it is placed in another function.

The next unique function block is the shared function. This function has to be executed before inti or any other function for that matter. You will want to use this function when you want a constant in your function. But, then the constant will need to be declared before each function is carried out.

Finally, you have the *any function*. This function is executed before every other function except when the init function is being used.

Sending Wei

A contract will not only have currency sent, but it will have the option of sending Ether to itself. The msg. Value function will contain the amount of wei that needs to be delivered along with the contract. When you want to send wei to someone else, you will use the send function.

Cryptocurrency

Syntax

Send (user address, amount of Ether)

Data structures that are persistent

A persistent data structure will be declared by using the data declaration function. By using this, you are allowing for the declaration of tuples and arrays.

Example

Data twoDimArray [] []

In this example, you will be declaring an array of tuples. The tuple that is being declared will have two items each.

Data array with tuples [] (item1, item2)

Each variable will be persistent throughout the execution of the contract. This is not going to matter what function is being called on by the user.

Note: data is not going to be able to be declared from inside of a function. Instead, it should be placed at the top of the contract before there are any functions defined.

Example

Data array with tuples [] (item1, item2)

Def a function z (params):

...

Def a function y (params):

....

What will happen when you want to access the data in the structure that you have created? The answer is simple; the array will use a standard syntax that a tuple will be able to access by using a period coupled with the name of the value that you want to have access to. So, if you want to access the first item in the example above by using the second array address, you will have a series of code that looks similar to this:

X = self. Array with tuples [2]. Item1

From here the first item will be stored with the self. Array with tuples array by placing it in x.

Note: you need to have the self-declaration function for the contract to understand what you

Cryptocurrency

are referencing with the array with tuples structure that has been placed in the contract.

Self. Storage []: Ethereum will have a supply of persistent key-value stores that are known as self-storage. These self-storage functions will be used with older contracts for simplicity. In the end, these keys will be placed in brackets while being set to equal the value that you want it to be equal.

Example

Self.storage [y] = a

So, when this function is called forward, a will be returned. If you want to use a simple storage then this function will be helpful, but if you are using are using a more significant contract, then it is recommended that you use the use of data – that is if you are using a key value storage.-

Hashing

The serpent will make it to where you can use three hash functions. These hash functions are:

RIPEMD-160

SHA3

SHA-256

The function that takes all of the parameters from a and s will make it to where a is the array of elements that need to be hashed while s is the size of the array that is being hashed.

Example:

Your array consists of five numbers [3,5, 2,4, 5] and you will use SHA-256 to hash the array.

Def main (d)

Bleh = array (5)

Bleh[0]=3

Bleh [1] = 5

Bleh [2] = 2

Bleh [3] = 4

Bleh[4] = 5

Return (sha256 (bleh, items = 5))

Cryptocurrency

Your result will be:

[92958224028375895182299457531563411438064489999392516673354862354350599884701L]

The function definitions are:

X= sha3 (a size= s) when using SHA3

X = sha256(a size = a) when working with SHA-256

X = ripemd160(a size= s) for the function RIPEMD-160

Note: if there is any input into your hash function then it can be seen by someone that is on the blockchain. So, when it comes to trying to keep secrets between you and someone else, the hash values need to be computed off of the blockchain so that only the hash value is put on the blockchain. In doing this, you have to decode the secret that is placed in the hash; so you should be sending the nonce as well as the text to the blockchain before it is rehashed and then compared to the hash value that was stored previously.

Random number generator

To do a random number generation, you need to have access to a previous block so it can be used as a seed. From there you will use modulus to make sure that the random number is coming from the appropriate range.

Example

Def main (a):

Raw = block. Prevhash

If raw < 0:

Raw = 0 − raw:

Return (raw%a)

Note: you need to make sure that your raw number is positive!

If you want your lowest number to be something other than zero, you need to add that number to your random number generator. It is at this point that you will be referencing a previous block. To do that, you need to make sure that there are current blocks that you are will be able to reference. When working with the Ethereum's

Cryptocurrency

blockchain,this is not going to be a big deal because you can build a block on your genesis block so that you have a previous block.

As you test your block, you will need to check more blocks. This will help in giving your more Ether should the tester run out of Ether. To do this, you will need to use the syntax that you see below.

s. mine (n=1 coinbase = tester.ao)

n will be the number of blocks that need to be mined; coin base will be the tester's address where the mining will take place.

Note python code can work here, but in that case, s will refer to the current state of the blockchain. You are not going to be able to mine from inside a contract that was written with Serpent because the function needs to be used once you have created the state.

Gas

You have learned that smart contracts are basically little individual programs. Most programmers know that an infinite loop or having an inefficient code will cause problems with the system. Ethereum's network does not have a lot of computing power, which is why it is specifically designed to work with smart contracts. To make sure you are efficiently programming your system, the execution of a contract will require what is known as gas. This gas will be used in each operation that will happen inside of a transaction. Transactions are funded which eliminates any infinite loops that may occur.

As you are using the tester, you will need to send a random amount of gas to your contract; sending the gas will be free. But,whenever you execute contracts on the live blockchain, you need to make sure that you only spend the gas that you need! The best way for you to complete this task is to use the pyEtherum.tester which will use the variables. Block.gas_used. S will be the current state of the blockchain. The gas that a transaction use will be stored in the block that you are currently working on. Being that it is a tester, you will need to use the transactions that are on the block, but this will only count the gas that is used by your current transaction.

Cryptocurrency

Example

S =tester. State ()

Print (s.block. gas_used) #call1 = 0 gas

C= s.abi_contract (serpent_code)

Print (s. Block. Gas_used) #call 2 = 3016 gas

O= c.deposit (value = 1000, sender = tester.k0)

Print(o)

Print (s. Block.gas_used)#call 3= 3879 gas

As you see in the example above, you have three examples of how much gas is used. In the first call, you are not going to have any transactions going. Therefore, you will not be using any gas. But, when it comes to the second call, there is a contraction the blockchain, so 3016 gas was used.

Now,what if you decide you want to know how much gas the deposit command will use? You will be able to subtract how much gas was used in the third call from the gas in the second call.3879- 3016 = 863. That means that your gas parameter will be 863.

So, now that you know how much gas is being used for your transactions, you need to know how much you will be spending on gas. On the current blockchain, gas will cost around 10 Szabo per unit. However,the group will change whenever Ethereum changes. So, the total price of the contract will be equal to how much you will be spending on gas to complete your transaction.

Note: when a contract runs out of gas,the execution of the transaction will roll back so that it is like it never happened. But, gas and any value that you have sent to the contract or the mine is not going to be refunded.

The call stack

The maximum call stack for Ethereum is 1024. There are attackers that can call contracts with a stack that already exists. So, if a send function is called while it is at its maximum, then an exception will be created; but, the exception to the contract will keep going. So, there will be individual portions that will be skipped in the contract. To fix this issue, you will need to insert a string of code at the beginning of the function

Cryptocurrency

to make sure that the attacker does not skip any part of the contract.

Syntax:

If self.test_callstack() ! =1: return (-1)

From there a function will be created, and the syntax for that function will be def test_callstack(): return (1).

Since this function is created, the attacker that attempts to break the stack will cause the contract to not be executed.

Chapter Twelve:

Ethereum's Future

No one is sure what the future holds in store for Ethereum, but from what you have read in this book, it is evident that the future will be bright for the network!

Ethereum is continually developing and changing, and if you are not sure about investing with Ethereum, then you need to look at all of the new developments that are coming from the system and how much it has to offer you when it comes to how you can make money with it.

It is alright to be hesitant about investing with a new platform that is continually evolving because you do not know what it will do and, of course, you do not want to lose money to something that is not going to be around.

However, think about when the stock market first came around. People were hesitant about that too, but, it is still around to this day, and people are continually making money or losing it with the stock market.

It is all a game of figuring out where your niche is and how you can improve your skills so that you can beat the odds and make a profit. Just remember that you need to learn from your mistakes!

And, just because you do not make money right away does not mean that you should give up with Ethereum. Keep investing because you are bound to make money sooner or later! Especially with Ethereum developing the way that it is!

Bonus: Quick Tips and Tricks

Here are some quick tips and tricks that can help you make things easier when using Ethereum.

1. Secure your password

   Secure your Ethereum account with a unique password just as you would with your social media account and bank account. You don't want to compromise your money. Accounts with a simple and patterned password are more accessible to hackers. For example, one of the common passwords many people use is their birth date using numbers that correspond to the month, date, and year. DO NOT USE SIMPLE PASSWORDS. Use unique ones. A difficult password will keep attackers out of your account. A secure password contains letters, numbers, symbols, and must be at least 10 characters long.

The longer the password, the harder it is for attackers to know it. Of course, if you want to use a long password, you should remember what it is. You might want to write it down in a secret paper, or at least write down hints that will make you remember your password.

2. Your wallet must be encrypted

Cryptocurrency wallets are sensitive. They store information about the funds of your digital currency. There are many wallets available today. You must choose the one that has high protection level for the users. You can select the trusted wallets like MyEtherWallet.

3. Backup your wallet

Having a back-up for your wallet offers several benefits. With your wallet backed up, you can save your account in case there would be system failures.

Conclusion

Thank you for making it through to the end of *Cryptocurrency*, let's hope it was informative and able to provide you with all of the tools you need to achieve your goals whatever it may be.

Throughout the book, we taught you about how you can make money with Ethereum. Now, create an Ethereum account and start investing. There are a lot of things that Ethereum has to offer. And as it continually grows, we can expect it to be more advanced and secure in a way that it can change the future of the financial system.

While Ethereum has proved its worth, benefit, and advancement, many people are still skeptical about it. And, of course, we can't blame them. No one can ever tell the future of this digital currency. However, we can be confident that it will grow because more and more people are now trusting in this digital money.

Cryptocurrency

The next step is to pick which method you want to use the cryptocurrency Ether and its blockchain application. Using Ether will be similar to using Bitcoin, but it is still going to be different because it runs off of a different platform and it has its own set of protocols that have to be followed.

Even with the differences that Ethereum has from Bitcoin, it is still a platform that will allow you to make money. All that is left is for you to take advantage of the money-making opportunities that it provides!

Finally, if you found this book useful in any way, a review on Amazon is always appreciated!

Thank you and good luck!

Cryptocurrency

————— ❧❦❧ —————

How to Make Money with Bitcoin -
The Investor's Guide to Bitcoin Mining,
Trading, Blockchain, and Smart
Contracts

by

David Blake

Table of Contents

validity or interim quality. Trademarks that are mentioned are done without written consent and can in no way be considered an endorsement from the trademark holder.

The author of this book has taken careful measures to share vital information about the subject. May its readers acquire the right knowledge, wisdom, inspiration, and succeed.

Introduction

These days, bitcoin is continuously gaining popularity and public acceptance. Many people want to learn how Bitcoin works and hope to find their way to financial freedom. In fact, the majority of those who use bitcoin do not actually use it as a substitute for money. Instead, they see bitcoin as a lucrative investment, and for good reason. The value of bitcoin has been constantly increasing over the years. As of November 2017, the price of 1 bitcoin has reached more than USD 8,000, and it is only climbing higher. Although bitcoin is also subject to the usual fluctuations in price, if you look at its long-term price movement, it is easy to recognize that it is a very profitable investment.

Before any person can take advantage of what bitcoin offers, you need to have a good foundation and understanding of what bitcoin is really all about. The following chapters will teach you the ins and outs of bitcoin. You will learn more about Bitcoin and its brief history. You will also get knowledge about what cryptocurrency and blockchain technology are that you are going to be able to use for a wide variety of lucrative purposes in the near future.

Bitcoin is continuously improving. We will tackle what the pros and cons of using Bitcoin are to ensure you get started on the right foot. Knowing about these will help you avoid the common mistakes that many new investors make, and prosper where they have burnt out early. As you continue reading this book, you will be guided on how you can effectively make money through Bitcoin. Soon, you will understand why thousands of new investors put their trust in Bitcoin every single day.

Bitcoin's development has been really fascinating, in less than a decade it has grown from an online novelty into a world-changing economic powerhouse. No wonder why many people all around the globe are now trusting this new digital currency. To see where things might be going in the future, we will also discuss Bitcoin's likely future as well.

Chapter 1:

Bitcoin Basics

What is Bitcoin?

Bitcoin is a digital currency that is held and stored electronically. It functions as a substitute for money. It also has a decentralized network. This means that no central authority or government controls it. Remember, Bitcoin does not have a physical existence; it only exists online.

Bitcoin is the most popular and successful cryptocurrency in the world. As of November 22, 2017, the price of 1 Bitcoin is around $8,179 (USD).

Bitcoin is accepted and used by different merchants worldwide: The gaming platform, Steam, accepts bitcoins. The giant computer software, Microsoft, also accepts payment in bitcoins. The company engaged in space tourism known as Virgin Galactic also accepts bitcoins. Overstock and even some sellers on Shopify accept payments in bitcoins. Many individuals and merchants use Bitcoin. The good news is that with the increasing popularity of the Bitcoin cryptocurrency, more and more people and businesses are being open to the idea of using Bitcoin.

Cryptocurrency

The term *cryptocurrency* refers to a digital asset that is secured by cryptography. Cryptography is the process of securing information. The application of cryptography can be traced back to the time of the Second World War when it was important to ensure that information and communication between and among the parties are secured and would not be disclosed to the enemy. After some time, cryptography found its application in cryptocurrency by converting information into codes that are almost uncrackable, which can then be used to track purchases and all other transactions. To date, there are more than 900 cryptocurrencies that have already been created. Creating a new cryptocurrency is easy. In fact, a basic knowledge in C++ will allow you to generate your own cryptocurrency in just a few days. The problem is that it is not easy to effectively promote a cryptocurrency, much less to convince people to take interest and use or invest in your cryptocurrency.

You can consider cryptocurrency as the primary Internet money since it is stored and transacted online. Keep in mind that cryptocurrencies like Bitcoin are not considered legal tender. Therefore, they are not a medium of payment that can be used by a debtor to compel his creditor to accept payment, except if payment in cryptocurrency is stated in the contract. The good news is that although cryptocurrencies are not considered as legal tender, many individuals and businesses are still open to the use of cryptocurrencies like Bitcoin.

Brief history of Bitcoin

In August of 2008, the domain name, *bitcoin.org*, was registered. After a few months, a paper entitled *Bitcoin: A Peer-to-Peer Electronic Cash System* was published on a cryptography mailing list under the pseudonym, Satoshi Nakamoto. In January 2009, Bitcoin was finally introduced in the market.

Cryptocurrency

It was also Satoshi Nakamoto who mined the first block of the Bitcoin chain, known as the *genesis block*, and for which he received 50 bitcoins. One of the early supporters of Bitcoin was a man named Hal Finney. On the same day when Bitcoin was released, Mr. Finney downloaded the bitcoin software, and for which he received 10 bitcoins from Satoshi Nakamoto. Said transaction is considered the very first bitcoin transaction in history. Even to this day, the true identity of Satoshi Nakamoto remains a mystery.

It is estimated that Satoshi Nakamoto had mined millions worth of bitcoins before he disappeared from the public. Some say that Satoshi Nakamoto was Hal Finney himself, while others claim that Nakamoto was composed of a group of computer experts. There have been many views and theories on the true identity of Satoshi Nakamoto yet no one can absolutely guarantee the real person or people behind one of the world's revolutionizing technologies, Bitcoin.

Another interesting bitcoin transaction in history was the purchase of two pizzas for 10,000 bitcoins. Back then, Bitcoin did not have a huge value. However, Bitcoin has grown significantly over time. A classic example to illustrate this point is this: If only you had invested even just $500 in bitcoins back in 2009 or 2010, then you would have been a multimillionaire by now. The good news is that even today, the price of bitcoin is continuously increasing.

Blockchain

The blockchain, originally referred to as *block chain*(two words), is the backbone technology of Bitcoin. The block is a form of a public, decentralized, and distributed ledger. It also has high security. Every block or record on the chain is connected to a previous block. This means that any change or modification made to any block will affect the whole blockchain system. This connection between and among the different blocks on the chain ensures that all records are legitimate, honest, and secure.

In a blockchain, the records are distributed and spread across a vast network of computers. To successfully attack a blockchain, a hacker will need to have at least 51% of the total hash rate or computing power of the entire network. This is the concept of the 51% attack. Since Bitcoin has a very broad network, it also has a very high hash rate, which makes it virtually unhackable.

The Bitcoin blockchain is a public blockchain, which means that all bitcoin transactions are verifiable and viewable to everyone. This is to ensure fairness and integrity of the records.

Be aware that in bitcoin's blockchain system, confirmed transactions could no longer be canceled, altered, modified, or withdrawn. Hence, be very careful with every input that you make.

The blockchain technology is not only applicable to bitcoin. Many experts have discovered that the blockchain technology can actually be used for other financial services, and even for non-financial purposes.

Is there a private blockchain?

When people talk about the blockchain technology, they always perceive it as something that is public because this is how bitcoin's blockchain is structured. What many people are not aware of is that there is also another kind of blockchain known as a private blockchain. Unlike a public blockchain, a private blockchain has a central authority or organization that has control and power over the entire blockchain system. This specialized authority or group can change, add, and remove, transactions over the blockchain network even without the consent of everyone in the network. As you can see, this is something that can be abused. This kind of blockchain is good for the use of private companies or between and among known and trusted parties. This kind of blockchain is not recommended for any cryptocurrency as it can be used to unduly influence the records. Fortunately, bitcoin's blockchain system is a public blockchain, so you can rest assured that all the records are fair, safe, and genuine.

Bitcoin transaction process

How does a bitcoin transaction work? There are three main elements of a transaction, namely: The input, recipient's wallet address, and the amount. Let us take a closer look at them one by one:

➢ Input

Before you can start sending bitcoins to anyone, you must first have bitcoins in your bitcoin wallet. Thisis referred to as the input.

It is the bitcoins in the bitcoin wallet of the sender. For example, if A will send 10 bitcoins to B, then A needs to have at least 10 bitcoins in his bitcoin wallet.

➢ Recipient's wallet address

This refers to the wallet address where you will send bitcoins. You should know your recipient's bitcoin wallet address. A wallet address is like a string of random letters and numbers.

➢ Amount

This simply refers to the amount that is involved in the transaction. In our example, the amount involved is 10 bitcoins. Make sure that you input the correct amount as it is impossible to cancel a transaction once it has been confirmed.

Smart contracts

Smart contracts are computer protocols that function to ensure, verify, and facilitate the negotiation and performance of contracts between the parties. Once certain conditions are met, then smart contracts will handle the execution of a contract. Although smart contracts are only known to execute simple tasks only, you can use numerous smart contracts to handle more complicated tasks.

Bitcoin is not known for its ability to use and handle smart contracts. Among the many cryptocurrencies out there, Ethereum is the one that is known for making use of smart contracts. The Bitcoin protocol has already evolved and now supports the use of smart contracts. Although the functionality of bitcoin's smart contracts is not as programmable as it is on Ethereum, certain functionality can still be made using bitcoin scripting.

Smart contracts are self-executing contracts. As long as the terms and conditions are met, then you can rest assured that the contract will be executed to the letter. Smart contracts allow transactions to take place even between anonymous parties.

The idea of a smart contract can be traced back in 1994. A proposal was made by a computer scientist named, Nick Szabo. He was also the inventor of Bit Gold, a type of virtual currency which was introduced in 1998. Yes, bitcoin was not the first cryptocurrency that was introduced in the market. According to Szabo, "These new securities are formed by combining securities (such as bonds) and derivatives (options and futures) in a wide variety of ways. Very complex term structures for payments can now be built into standardized contracts and traded with low transaction costs, due to computerized analysis of these complex term structures."

Other cryptocurrencies

There are more than 900 different cryptocurrencies that have already been created, and new cryptocurrencies are continuously being introduced in the market. Although there are many different kinds of cryptocurrencies out there, only a few can attract the market's attention and interest. Bitcoin remains to be the number one cryptocurrency in the world. In fact, it is the leading standard that all other cryptocurrencies have been categorized as *altcoins*, which is short for alternative coins. Let us take a look at some of the notable altcoins in the world:

➢ Ethereum

Ethereum was launched in 2015. It is currently the second most successful cryptocurrency in the world next to bitcoin. Some people even claim that Ethereum will soon overtake Bitcoin, although this seems far from happening. Ethereum uses smart contracts and Distributed Applications. Ethereum applications run using Ethereum's own platform cryptographic token known as *ether*. As of November 22, 2017, the price of 1 ether is around USD 365.

➢ Litecoin

Litecoin is not a new player in the cryptocurrency market. It was launched in 2011 and became one of the early competitors of bitcoin. Litecoin functions just like bitcoin, and it aims to be the "better" version of bitcoin. It claims to have a higher block generation rate, which means that it can confirm transactions much faster than bitcoin. There is also a growing number of businesses that accept Litecoin. As of November 22, 2017, the price of 1 Litecoin is around USD 70.

Cryptocurrency

➢ Ripple

Unlike other cryptocurrencies that seem to take the place of banks, Ripple actually works mutually with banks. It "enables banks to settle cross-border payments in real time, with end-to-end transparency, and at lower costs." It was launched in 2012 and is slowly gaining market capitalization. As of November 22, 2017, the price of 1 Ripple is around USD 0.23.

➢ Zcash

Zcash was launched in the latter part of 2016. This is how Zcash defines itself: "If Bitcoin is like http for money, Zcash is https," and the reason is that Zcash offers more privacy than Bitcoin. When you use Zcash, you will be offered a choice to use *shielded transactions*. Using advanced cryptography, shielded transactions will make private the details as to the sender, recipient, and even the amount involved in a transaction. As of November 22, 2017, the price of 1 Zcash is around USD 290.

➢ Monero

Monero was launched in 2014. It has drawn lots of interest in the cryptocurrency community. In fact, it is the only cryptocurrency that is purely donation-based. Its main focus is on decentralization and scalability. It also allows its users to enjoy improved privacy by using its unique feature known as *ring signatures*. When you use ring signatures, a legitimate transaction that you make is mixed up with fake or invalid transactions. Hence, when people look at the public blockchain, it will be hard to tell which transaction is valid and those that are not real. This way the real transaction (your transaction) will be "hidden." As of November 22, 2017, the price of 1 Monero is around USD 146.

There are many other cryptocurrencies in the world. The list above is only to give you an idea of other famous cryptocurrencies. As you can see, to compete with bitcoin, altcoins have additional features to make them appear more valuable. Gone are the days when you can just introduce a cryptocurrency in the market and expect a good following. To attract attention and interest, you need to focus on effective promotion and give value to the market. Still, it is worth stressing the fact that among all the cryptocurrencies in the world, Bitcoin remains the be the number one and most successful cryptocurrency, with a price of around USD 8,179 as of November 22, 2017 — and its price is continuously increasing.

Legality of using bitcoin

Although Bitcoin is unregulated and decentralized, it does not mean that the state cannot impose regulations or restrictions on its use. After all, a state has the primary responsibility of protecting its people and promoting the general welfare. Generally, the use of bitcoins is legal but there are a few states like Ecuador and Bolivia where the use of bitcoin and other cryptocurrencies is outlawed.

It is not hard to understand why the use of bitcoin and other cryptocurrencies is considered illegal in some states. Due to the level of anonymity enjoyed by cryptocurrency users, it can be used in the commission of crimes like money laundering. Although most states do not totally outlaw the use of Bitcoin, certain security measures may be imposed, such as the Know Your Customer (KYC) policy, and others. Still, there are states like Singapore that do not impose any form of regulation on the use of Bitcoins or any other cryptocurrency. Before you start using bitcoins, it is suggested that you check the laws and rules of your state on the matter. The good news is that more and more states are being open to the idea of using cryptocurrency. In fact, Russia which previously outlawed the use of bitcoins is now one of the supporters of bitcoin. As time goes by, more and more people are being open and accept the use of Bitcoin.

How to earn bitcoins

Before you can make money with bitcoins, you should first have your own bitcoins. So, how do you earn bitcoins? The best way to earn your first bitcoins for investing is by buying bitcoins. There are hot wallets like Coinbase and coins.ph that will allow you to purchase bitcoins instantly using your Visa or Master card. You can also buy bitcoins from local and online bitcoin exchanges. You should be very careful when buying bitcoins. Do not forget that the price of bitcoin fluctuates significantly in a short period of time. Before you make any buy order, be sure to check the current price of bitcoin. Another good place to buy bitcoins is from cryptocurrency trading platforms. This means that you will have to sign up for a free account with a bitcoin trading broker. Do not worry; the signing up process can be completed in as fast as two minutes.

There are other ways to earn bitcoins, such as by mining, gambling, and others. All these are discussed in more detail later in the book. Another way to earn bitcoin is to request it as a mode of payment. After all, bitcoin is a substitute for money. This is easy to do, especially if you have an e-commerce or online business. Just give your bitcoin address to the customers, and you will be able to receive payments at any time. Still, when it comes to investing in bitcoins, the best and easiest way is simply to buy bitcoins just as anyone who wants to invest in stocks would have to buy stocks. It is worth repeating that before you buy bitcoins, you should first know the current price of bitcoin to be sure that you are getting a fair deal. There are many sites online that sell bitcoins at a very high price.

There are people who want to buy bitcoins using PayPal. The way to do this is by using another service known as Virwox. You should know that this is not a good way to buy bitcoins because the process is very expensive. Therefore, although this may seem convenient to you, this is not a suggested method.

Is it for you?

There are many ways to make money, and making money with bitcoin is probably not for everyone. Again, even though bitcoin continues to prove itself as a profitable investment, it is still an investment. This means that it is still vulnerable to certain risks, including the risk of losing all your money. If you are not the type who is willing to take risks, then bitcoin might not be for you. If you are willing to exert some hard work in research and are ready to face some risks, then investing in bitcoin might just be the best investment that you can make, for it is something that can completely change your life for the better.

Chapter 2:

Pros and Cons of Using Bitcoin

Pros

➤ Cannot be manipulated

Bitcoin has a decentralized network. It is not under the control of any central authority or government. Hence, it is not subject to any form of undue influence or manipulation. In fact, even the founder of Bitcoin, Satoshi Nakamoto, cannot alter or remove the records on bitcoin's blockchain. You can rest assured that the record of transactions is fair and free from any form of manipulation.

➤ Lower cost

The bitcoin blockchainis designed in a way that it effectively removes the middleman. You do not have to worry about banking fees or any other third-party fee. You can send and receive bitcoins over the bitcoin network without having to rely on any other service provider. This effectively cuts down your cost, especially if you intend to send or receive bitcoins on a regular basis.

➢ Anonymity

Bitcoin users enjoy a high level of anonymity. When you make a transaction, whether sending or receiving bitcoin, your name and other personal details will not be revealed. The only record that will appear on the blockchain would be your bitcoin wallet address, the bitcoin wallet address of the recipient, the amount involved, and a time stamp. All personal information will be kept private and confidential.

➢ Quick transactions

Unlike transacting with banks where you may have to wait for days for a check or transaction to clear, bitcoin transactions only takes a few minutes to complete. If you are willing to pay a small mining fee, then the transaction can be completed almost instantly. Such quick transaction feature is one of the main highlights of using bitcoins.

➢ Round the clock availability

The bitcoin network does not close. It is open and available 24/7, even during holidays. Feel free to send and receive bitcoin at any time you want. Unlike transacting with banks that are only available every weekday, the bitcoin network is always available.

➢ Profitable

Investing in bitcoin can be highly profitable. Let me remind you of a classic example: Had you invested even just $500 in bitcoin way back in 2009 or 2010, then you would have been a multimillionaire by now. Had you invested in bitcoin early in 2017, then you would have profited by more than 100% of your total investment by now. The gold need is that despite the already high value of bitcoin, it remains to be a lucrative investment. According to some experts, the value of bitcoin can be expected to increase by more than 300% within the next two years.

Cryptocurrency

➢ Convenient

Using bitcoins is very convenient. Everything happens online with just a few clicks of a mouse. You do not have to drive and visit your bank; all that you need to focus access the Internet using your computer or a mobile device, and you can make transactions easily and quickly.

Cons

➢ High volatility

The price of bitcoin fluctuates rapidly and significantly. It is not uncommon for its price to experience an increase or decrease of 10% in just 24 hours. This is one of the reasons why there are investors who are cautious of investing in bitcoin but it is also the high volatility of bitcoin that makes it an attractive investment. Due to its high volatility, high price surges become possible.

➢ Technology risk

Although bitcoin is considered a good technology, there is a risk that a more competitive cryptocurrency may soon hit the market in such a way that bitcoin will lose its position as the number of cryptocurrency in the world.

It should also be noted that bitcoin's network runs on a very high hash rate considering the multitude of computer networks connected to it. There is a risk that the technology behind bitcoin may not be able to handle too much hash rate in the long run. Although bitcoin appears to be very advanced, it is still a fact that bitcoin, as well as the blockchain technology, is a fairly new kind of technology.

➢ Security risk

Although the blockchain prides itself on a high level of security, it does not mean that it is absolutely invulnerable to all forms of attack. There are also some experts who claim that the 51‰ attack concept is not absolute. In fact, since the bitcoin network is connected with one another, a successful attack on a single node or block can adversely affect the entire bitcoin blockchain. There are also some bitcoin wallets that have been hacked and compromised. When you use bitcoins, you should be aware of the best practices on how you can keep your bitcoin wallet safe and secure.

➢ Legal risk

At present, only a few states consider the use of bitcoin and other cryptocurrencies to be illegal, and only a few impose stringent regulations. This does not mean that governments will no longer regulate its use in the future. According to experts, governments may soon take stricter measures if more people switch to bitcoin and begin to stop using legal tender money (the money issued by the government). This is because such instance can cause a significant drop in the price of a state's official currency. This is a simple application of the law on supply and demand. If people turn to bitcoin and the demand for the state's official currency decreases, then you can expect for its price to drop, which will not be good for the economy. Also, due to the enhanced privacy and security enjoyed by bitcoin users, the state can take preventive and protective measures, especially if it has good reasons to believe that bitcoin is also being used for the commission of illegal activities.

Chapter 2: Pros and Cons of Using Bitcoin

➤   Market risk

Whether investing in stocks, realty, or cryptocurrency, one of the crucial factors to look for is the market. It is not just the price of bitcoin that is highly volatile, even the market behavior is also hard to predict. If the market suddenly changes its mind or preference and switches to another cryptocurrency or stops using cryptocurrency, then this can hurt the price of bitcoin.

Another common market risk is when investors are in a state of panic. For example, when China declared to close down all its local cryptocurrency exchanges, there was panic in the market, and investors cashed out their positions by making sell orders thinking that the price of bitcoin would take a massive drop. This resulted in a more significant decrease in the price of bitcoin that it was supposed to be. As you can see, how the market reacts to changes can have a serious effect on the price of bitcoin.

Cryptocurrency

➤   Competition

There is a tight level of competition among the different cryptocurrencies in the market. Not to mention, new cryptocurrencies are also being introduced in the market, and these cryptocurrencies also offer value and additional features. Although competition may be considered healthy as it compels businesses to improve and maintain a decent quality, it can also cause businesses or cryptocurrencies to lose their share in the market. To remain a profitable investment, bitcoin needs to maintain its edge and stay ahead of the competition.

The competition per se is not bad. In fact, it is an essential element in business to ensure the best quality of service. In the world of cryptocurrency, competition can be a problem as it can easily cause a certain cryptocurrency to lose market capitalization. It is quite surprising that although bitcoin does not offer additional value or features, it remains the number one cryptocurrency in the world.

Is it worth it?

When making any investment, you need to weigh the pros and cons and see if it is worth taking. This book teaches bitcoin but does not promote it in any way. Now, by simply looking at and comparing the pros and cons of bitcoin, as well as analyzing the things that are taking place in the market, it is not difficult to tell that bitcoin is worth taking as an investment. It has a high-profit potential. In fact, its profit potential is way higher than the usual investment opportunities like stocks, bonds, and realty. The good news is that the probability of making a profit is high. This is another thing that makes investing in bitcoin attractive. Unlike the regular kind of investment, if the profit potential is high, you can expect that the risk is also high. This is not how it works with bitcoin. When you invest in bitcoin, you know that you take ownership of something that many people consider as valuable. Another benefit is that most people believe that the value of bitcoin will continue to increase.

If you are still hesitant whether you should put your money in bitcoin or not, you can just test it for some time. Simply invest a small amount and

Cryptocurrency

see what happens. The important thing is to take action and grab the opportunity while it is still there. The truth is that some people in the world are earning lots of profit simply by investing their money in bitcoin. While bitcoin is still considered a hot topic and continuously draws attention, it is the best time to take advantage of it and rake in serious money.

Chapter 3:

Bitcoin Wallets

Before you can start to use bitcoins, you need a place where you can store them. You need to have a bitcoin wallet. There are many types of bitcoin wallets, and you need to understand their differences so that you will know which bitcoin wallet will best suit your needs.

Different types of Bitcoin wallets

Basically, there are two main categories of a bitcoin wallet: a hot wallet and a cold wallet. A hot wallet refers to the kind of bitcoin wallet that exists online or on the web, while a cold wallet is a kind of bitcoin wallet that exists offline. On the one hand, since a hot wallet exists online, it is more convenient to use than a cold wallet. On the other hand, a cold wallet offers more security than a hot wallet since it is not exposed to the Internet.

Cold and hot wallets are further divided into different types. Let us take a look at the specific types of bitcoin wallets:

➤ Web wallet

Also known as an online or Internet wallet, a web wallet is a kind of hot wallet that you can use. This is also the most common wallet used by a majority of bitcoin users. A good example of a web wallet is Coinbase.

➤ Mobile wallet

A mobile wallet is just like a web wallet, but it is something that you can download on your mobile device. It is also a form of a hot wallet. Many web wallets are considered mobile wallets. A mobile wallet comes in the form of a downloadable application. There are many hot wallet sites that you can access using your mobile device.

➤ Desktop wallet

This is also referred to as a computer wallet. This is a kind of cold wallet where you store your bitcoins in a computer. Although usually called as a desktop wallet, it does not necessarily have to be a desktop computer. A laptop computer will do just fine.

Keep in mind that when you use a desktop wallet, you should not connect your computer to the Internet. The reason is that connecting your computer to the web will expose it to risks of getting hacked or compromised. There are many hackers and scammers online who are constantly looking for their next victim. You also do not need to use a new computer. An old computer with a well-functioning operating system will do just fine. Keep in mind that before you use it as a cold wallet, it is strongly advised that you reformat it to ensure that it is free of bugs and viruses.

➢ Hardware wallet

A hardware wallet is another kind of cold wallet. It is similar to a desktop wallet but instead of storing your bitcoins in a computer, you keep them in some form of hardware, such as a USB device. Again, be sure that the hardware where you intend to keep your bitcoins should be free of bugs and viruses. Hence, if you intend to use an old

USB device, then it is best to reformat it before you use it as a cold wallet.

> Paper wallet

A paper wallet is another popular kind of cold wallet. It is called a paper wallet because you keep and print your private keys on paper. It is suggested to have several copies and store them in a safe place.

Which type of bitcoin wallet should you use?

There is no hard and fast rule as to which bitcoin wallet you should use. The thing is to strike a good balance between convenience as offered by a hot wallet, and the security offered by a cold wallet. If you think that you will be sending and/orreceiving bitcoins regularly, then you might want to use a hot wallet. If you just want to store bitcoins for a long time in the form of an investment, then you may want to use a cold wallet. There are also bitcoin users who use both types of wallets at the same time. You can use a hot wallet for your day-to-day transactions and also keep a cold wallet for a long-term investment.

When you use a cold wallet, be sure to use something that has a good quality. If it gets broken, then it may be impossible to recover your bitcoins. Also, be sure to keep your cold wallet in a safe place. If it gets stolen, then you may no longer be able to recover your bitcoins. As you can see, even a cold wallet has its risks. It is also worth noting that many bitcoin users are already satisfied with a hot wallet. The good news is that the security offered by trusted and reliable hot wallets have already developed over time.

Bitcoin wallet protection tips

Here are notable tips to improve and ensure the security of your bitcoin wallet:

➢ Enhanced password

Your password is the first and main line of defense against hackers. Therefore, it is of primary importance that you use a strong password. But, what makes a strong password? There are certain guidelines for you to remember: Use a password that is hard to predict. Do not use your name or birth date as your password. Also, the longer your password is, the better. A common mistake is to only use the minimum number of characters. Also, you should combine upper and lower cases. You should also add some symbols and numbers to further increase the security of your account. It is also suggested that you update (change) your password from time to time.

➢ Request for a new wallet address

A single bitcoin wallet can generate multiple wallet addresses. Over the blockchain, your name or your bitcoin wallet itself will not be shown. It is only your bitcoin wallet address that will be revealed. You can request for a new bitcoin wallet address with just a click of a mouse, and this is free of charge. To minimize your exposure which, in turn, will minimize your risks, you should make it a habit of requesting for a new wallet address each time you make a transaction.

➢ Check if the page is secure

Before you key in your password or any sensitive information, check if the page is secure. This is easy to do: Simply look at the URL bar, and you should see a green padlock and/or the word "Secure." This signifies that it is safe to enter sensitive information like your bitcoin wallet address. This is a preventive measure against phishing sites or sites that duplicate a legitimate website to steal information.

➤ Avoid accessing your bitcoin wallet over a public Wi-Fi

Although a public Wi-Fi can be very convenient to use, it is not advisable when you want to access your bitcoin wallet. Connecting to a public Wi-Fi can be risky. Some hackers take advantage of public Wi-Fis. If you just want to surf the web, then there is nothing wrong with using a public Wi-Fi, but if you want to use access and manage your bitcoin wallet, especially if you need to key in sensitive information, then doing so over a public Wi-Fi is not a safe choice.

➤ Use multiple wallets

You have probably heard the saying, "Do not put all your eggs in one basket." The same advice is true when you use bitcoin wallets. Unfortunately, there have been reports of bitcoin wallets getting hacked. To minimize

Cryptocurrency

your risk, you should learn to spread your
risk by using multiple wallets. This is true,
especially if you are using a hot wallet. For
example, instead of storing 3 bitcoins in a
single hot wallet, store 1 bitcoin in a Coinbase
wallet, another 1 bitcoin in another hot wallet
like GreenAddress, and the remaining 1
bitcoin in a cold wallet.

➤ Keep your cold wallet in a safe place

Although cold wallets have a higher security
since they are not connected to the Internet,
they are still vulnerable to being stolen or
destroyed. Make sure to keep your cold wallet
in a safe place.

Chapter 4:

Make Money

L et us look at the different ways to make money with bitcoin. In fact, the main reason why many people are attracted to bitcoin is that of the amount of money that they can earn. The more bitcoins that you have, the more cash you can make.

Free faucet

This is the easiest way to earn your first bitcoins. If you are new to bitcoins and just want to experience having your own bitcoins, then you can take advantage of free faucets. A faucet will give you a small amount of bitcoin for free. You can find countless of bitcoin faucets online. You cannot expect to get rich simply by relying on faucets. A bitcoin faucet usually gives out a small amount of bitcoins on a regular basis. On average, you can expect to earn around 0.00000100 bitcoins per hour. This is not really an effective way to earn money, but it is a good way to make you earn your first bitcoins quickly and easily without any investment.

Bitcoin mining

Before any block is added to the chain, the transaction must first be confirmed and verified by miners. A miner receives a reward for mining. Mining is important to introduce a new block into the system. Without mining, transactions will remain unconfirmed and will not be completed. Since miners earn bitcoins as a reward, mining is also a good way to earn more bitcoins, which you can then convert into cash. There are generally two ways three ways to mine for bitcoins: (1) You can mine using your own computer; (2) You can mine using a hardware; and (3) You can mine using cloud mining.

Mining using your own computer is no longer suggested since you will most likely spend more money on electricity than the amount of bitcoins that you can earn for mining. To earn a significant amount of bitcoins, you need to have a higher hash mining power. To do this, you have two choices: mine using a hardware or over the cloud.

Chapter 4: Make Money

➤ Hardware mining

Mining using your computer alone is not enough. To make a good profit, you need to use a hardwareto increase your hash rate, which will allow you to earn more bitcoins. If you choose to do hardware mining, you need to purchase a good hardware for mining. Now, there are many different choices of hardware that you can choose from. Of course, a hardware that will give you more mining power will be more expensive. When you mine with a hardware, you still have to use your computer. Therefore, hardware mining means mining using your computer and a hardware at the same time.

The drawback to hardware mining is the issue of overheating. Since you will have to mine for hours on a regular basis using your computer and mining hardware, overheating can be a problem. Worse, it can break your computer and your hardware in the long run, which would mean additional expenses for you. If you intend to use hardware mining, you will have to follow a certain schedule for mining and always give time for your computer and mining hardware to cool down.

Cryptocurrency

> Cloud mining

Cloud mining is the type of bitcoin mining that is getting popular these days. With cloud mining, you will no longer have to buy a hardware. In fact, you do not even have to turn on your computer just to mine for bitcoins. When you use cloud mining, a mining company will do all the work for you. All that you need to do is wait for the mining company to send your bitcoins to your wallet. A good example of a cloud mining company is Genesis Mining. Normally, you will have to pay a mining company a certain amount. For example, deposit/pay 1 bitcoin and get 0.08 bitcoins every week. This will depend upon the agreement that you have with the mining company. There are also mining companies that will allow you to buy as many hash power rate as you want, and they will give you the expected equivalent bitcoins that you can get from them, depending on the number of the hash rate that you purchase.

Okay, so this looks like the best deal. But, what is the drawback, if any? The drawback is that what the mining company shows you is usually just the expected return and not the actual return that you will get. Hence, even if a mining company says that you can expect to get 0.08 bitcoins every week, you may end up only receiving 0.05 per week. Be sure that the terms and conditions of the contract are clear to you before you spend any real money. Also, be careful of scammers online. There have been reports where investors do not receive any bitcoins at all from a mining company. Be sure to work only with trusted and reliable mining company. You are expected to always do your research and pay attention to the latest ratings and reviews of a mining company before you deposit real money/cryptocurrency in your account.

Is bitcoin mining still profitable? It depends. The problem with mining bitcoins is that it will take time for you to recover your investment. Most experts suggest that if you are serious about earning money with bitcoin, then the best way is for you to study and learn how to invest in and trade bitcoin.

Bitcoin gambling

If you are fond of casino gambling, then bitcoin offers excellent online casino experience. In fact, bitcoin has its own gambling game known as Dice. Why would you want to gamble with bitcoin? Aside from the fact that there are many bitcoin casinos online, there are other good reasons on why you would want to gamble using bitcoin. Unlike other online casinos, you can deposit and withdraw bitcoin almost instantly. As for withdrawal, you will usually receive your bitcoins in your wallet in just a few minutes. In case you are withdrawing a big amount, you can still expect to receive your withdrawal in less than 24 hours. Normally, when you play casino online and withdraw funds to your bank, it will take days for a single transaction to be completed. With bitcoin, transactions get confirmed and completed quickly.

Most bitcoin casinos also have a provably fair system. What it does is to let you ensure that the outcome of a game is fair and without any form of bias or undue influence.

Bitcoin casinos also offer live casinos where you will be served by a live, beautiful, and professional dealer. Whether you want to play baccarat, blackjack, or roulette, you will definitely find a dealer for you. Most live casinos also gave a chat feature, which will allow you to talk with the dealer in real time. This way you can be sure that the games are not pre-recorded and that everything is actually happening in real time.

Still, casino gambling is not an advisable way to make money with bitcoin considering that most gamblers lose their money quickly or in the long run. If you think that you have a system that can beat the casino's house edge or if you simply want to try your luck, then bitcoin casinos will definitely give you a convenient and exciting experience.

Bitcoin trading

Bitcoin trading, or more specifically, cryptocurrency trading, is the most popular way to make money with bitcoin quickly. This works just like the typical forex, but you will have to deal with different cryptocurrencies. Therefore, this approach requires a good amount of research and analysis.

Another form of trading is binary options trading. There are many sites online that will allow you to do binary trading with bitcoin. Binary options are the closest that you can get to casino gambling as you can trade binary in as fast as one minute or even 30 seconds. Although you can still make money with binary options, it is not as easy as it may seem. In fact, themajority of people who invest in binary options end up losing their money. If you ever intend to focus on binary trading, then be sure to learn and use proper strategies.

Bitcoin investing

This is the most common way to make money with bitcoin. The main factor that creates the profit is the increasing price of bitcoin. For example, if had you invested in bitcoin in the early part of 2017, then you would have gained a profit of more than 100‰ of your original investment by now. The most common strategy when investing in bitcoin is the buy and hold strategy. As the name implies, you simply have to buy bitcoins, and then hold on to them as you wait for their price to increase. You can then sell them for profit in the future. If you do not want to get too technical, then this strategy is the one for you. Had you applied this strategy way back in 2010 even with just a $400 investment, then you would have been a multimillionaire by now.

Chapter 4: Make Money

Investing in bitcoin is actually very easy to do. All that you need is to get a bitcoin wallet, buy bitcoins, keep them in your wallet, and wait for the price of bitcoin to increase. This is all about the common principle that states: "Buy low, sell high."

The price of bitcoin can fluctuate significantly even within a 24-hour timeline. Therefore, proper timing should be observed before you make any buy order. A suggested way to do this is to study the recent trend of bitcoin and see if making a buy order at this very moment would be a good choice or should you wait for a few more hours. With enough research, you will be able to predict to theright time to buy bitcoins. Usually, the best time to make a buy order is before or immediately right after a certain promotion or event about bitcoin is made. The more positive attention is given to bitcoin, the more likely its price will increase. Hence, if you think the price of bitcoin will increase, then make a buy order; if you think that its price will decrease, then make a sell order.

Chapter 5:

Bitcoin Investing/Trading Strategies

Fundamental analysis

Fundamental analysis is also referred to as the lifeblood of investment. This is how essential this strategy is. The reason is that this strategy deals with the basics. As the name implies, it focuses on the fundamentals. When you deal with bitcoins and use fundamental analysis, you will have to examine and analyze the different factors that affect the price of bitcoin, such as market behavior, competition among the different cryptocurrencies, news updates, legalities, economy, latest trends and technological developments, among others.

No matter which strategy you use, fundamental analysis remains vital as it can be used to justify your investment decision. Fortunately, this strategy is something that you can apply and combine with another strategy. It always helps to know and understand what is going on in the bitcoin and cryptocurrency economy. The more that you understand the different factors that affect the price of bitcoin, the more easily you can predict its price movement.

So, before you make any trade or investment, take some time to analyze the situation. Look at the different factors that affect the price of bitcoin. When you do fundamental analysis, then you need to be ready to make some serious research. Again, the key to this strategy is to get as much basic information as you can. Once you have the fundamentals sorted out, then you will have a better view of the market. This will allow you to make a better investment or trading decision. You should also understand that the price of bitcoin does not fluctuate at random. It just so happens that many factors affect its price movement, but it is never left to chance. Therefore, by taking the time to understand these factors, you will be able to better predict its price behavior. Once you can foresee how its price will move, then you can take appropriate actions (buy or sell bitcoins) for profit.

If you see yourself as a serious investor or trader, then fundamental analysis should be a part of your everyday life. Always be updated on the news and learn as much as you can about everything that can be connected to bitcoin.

Fundamental analysis does not end with just getting the facts. Another vital step is for you to properly analyze the details that you have. Be careful not to be biased in your judgment. You should look at the facts from an unbiased and impartial perspective. This way you can have a better view of what is actually going on in the bitcoin market and identify the best move to take.

Technical analysis

This is a favorite approach of many investors and traders. Unlike fundamental analysis that deals with hard facts and numbers, technical analysis deals with graphs and charts. So, if you are more of a visual person, then this strategy is for you. The graphs and charts reflect the price movements of bitcoin. The concept behind this strategy is that the different factors that influence the price movements of bitcoin have their final effect on the price. Therefore, simply by analyzing the price movements and fluctuations, you also get to deal with all the other factors that affect bitcoin.

When you use technical analysis, you should learn to recognize and read patterns. It should be noted that patterns come and go. Nonetheless, they still happen from time to time. A common mistake committed by many traders is to see a pattern even when no pattern actually exists. Keep in mind that you should never force a pattern. Just because you look at a certain graph for more than 20 minutes does not mean that there is always a pattern or trend to be seen. If you are truly able to identify a certain trend, then you should take advantage of it. Even a random generator still forms patterns from time to time. The key to profit is to be able to identify a pattern and take advantage of it before it disappears.

Just like fundamental analysis, you can combine technical analysis with other strategies. Since technical analysis deals with graphs and charts, you can use this approach as a tool to get additional information. But, where do you get these graphs and charts? Ideally, it is your broker that should provide you with these helpful tools. If your broker does not provide the said graphs, then you can visit bitcoin and other cryptocurrency websites to see charts that show the price behavior of bitcoin, as well as other cryptocurrencies. Although there are people who believe that technical analysis alone is enough to provide you with all the information that you need to come up with a sound investment decision, this book encourages that you use technical analysis together with fundamental analysis.

Go with the flow

A few months ago, there was positive news about bitcoin that was featured on CNN. As can be expected, the price of bitcoin increased. After some time, there was news about China closing down its local cryptocurrency exchanges, and the price of bitcoin dropped. As you can see, the price movement of bitcoin is not that difficult to predict. A good news about bitcoin results in an increase in price, while a bad news on bitcoin tends to pull its price down. The key to the go with the flow strategy is to be updated on the latest news and respond accordingly. For example, if good news is being promoted about bitcoin, then you can expect for bitcoin's price to increase. Conversely, if there is any bad news about bitcoin, then it will most probably experience a decrease in value. By understanding the news, you will be able to tell the best time to make a buy or sell order. When it comes to investing and trading, proper timing is very important.

Averaging down

This strategy is an effective way to earn a significant amount of bitcoins. You need to be careful as this is considered an aggressive approach. Here is an example of how this strategy works: Let us say that the price of 1 bitcoin is equivalent to $5,000. You then make a buy order at the said price of $5,000. Now, let us assume that its price falls to $4,900, you then make another buy order at the said lower price of $4,900. Again, let us say that its price drops down to $4,750, you should make another buy order at the said price, and so on and so forth. By doing so, you get to buy it at a bargain each time you make a buy order. But, what a second, are you not buying a losing asset? In a way, yes, you are buying bitcoin while its price is falling down. This may be counter-intuitive. Try to imagine what will happen if its price shoots back up to its original price (the price when you first applied the strategy), then all the buy orders that you have made will turn into a profitable investment and experience a nice profit. This is actually the key to profit of the averaging down strategy. It takes advantage of the high volatility of bitcoin. Keep in mind to be careful when you use this approach as it is also possible for the price of bitcoin to experience a serious and constant downfall. Therefore, before you even use this strategy, be sure to do all the necessary research and analysis.

Quick sell

This strategy aims to earn a little bit of profit several times. You should be content with small gains. To make a decent income, you need to invest a huge amount of bitcoins. Here is an example of how this strategy works: Let us say that you have 1 bitcoin in your trading account. Once you see that the price of bitcoin increases during the day, then you make a sell order and enjoy your small profit from the transaction. Fortunately, the price of bitcoin fluctuates significantly within a 24-hour timeline. You simply have to repeat this process as much as you can. When you use this strategy, you have to avoid getting greedy. Instead, you should be content with a small amount of profit. This strategy also does not have any risk as you are sure to make a profit when you sell your bitcoins. All that you need to do is to have some bitcoins in your account, be patient, and sell your bitcoins for profit.

Is there a difference between investing and trading?

Many people use these terms synonymously. Whether investing and trading are the same or different depends on how you view it. For starters, you can say that trading entails a more active approach. After all, you can make multiple trades in a single day. Investing, on the other hand, entails a more passive approach where you simply buy something and wait for the right time to sell it for profit. When you invest in something, you will also trade it sooner or later to make a profit, and when you trade something, you also have to invest some money into the venture. From this perspective, then trading and investing can be considered closely similar. This book uses both terms synonymously. According to an expert, "It does not matter whether you see yourself as an investor or trader, the important thing is how much profit you make, if any."

Chapter 6:

Bitcoin Trading Broker

What to look for in a bitcoin trading broker

If you want to trade bitcoins, then you should work with a reliable and trusted broker. Doing a simple search online will give you a list of different brokers that seem to offer the same services. So, how do you know which broker will best suit your needs? Here are the standards to look for:

Latest ratings and reviews

Make sure to check the latest ratings and reviews of a trading broker before you deposit any money. You can easily do this by using your favorite search engine. Just type the name of the broker and add the word "reviews." Press the enter key, and the search engine results pages (SERP) will give you a list of related pages.

Cryptocurrency

Carefully read the reviews and take note of the dates when they were made. Also, it is not uncommon for brokers to hire a freelance writer to write a positive review about them, so do not just rely on a single website for reviews. Most legitimate reviews are those that also mention something negative about a broker. If a review seems too good to be true, then it is probably is. The more references and reviews that you read about a particular broker, the better.

Customer support

You should work with a broker that has a professional and responsive customer support. What are the ways that you can contact the support team? Is there a beer that you can call at any time or is there a live chat schedule? Most brokers can be contacted via email. Make sure that a broker's customer support team responds quickly. A good way to find out is to test it before you even make an account or before making a deposit. Just send a message to the support team and ask any legitimate question. Try to see how professionally they handle your inquiry, as well as how many days it will take them to resolve it.

Margin trading

Margin trading is where you can borrow bitcoins from your broker. In exchange, you will have to pay interest. Normally, a broker will allow you to margin trade more than 50‰ of your investment. This is a good way to earn a nice profit, especially if you do not have a big capital. Although margin trading is a good way to earn more profit, be cautious of using it as it can be a problem and a liability in the long run. If you ever make use of margin trading, then be sure to adapt a strategy that is suitable for it.

Mobile feature

Your broker's trading platform should be accessible on your mobile device. These days, the most convenient way to access the Internet is not with the use of a computer, but with your mobile phone. Do not worry; all trusted brokers have a mobile feature. The mobile version should also be easy to navigate, and it should allow you to access the important parts and features of the trading platform.

Cryptocurrency

Design and layout

Although not required, it still helps if the trading platform is professionally designed. It must have a layout that is easy and convenient to navigate. Simple yet professionally designed layouts are best for this. Navigating the platform should be easy and intuitive. The important parts of the trading platform should be properly sorted and easily accessible.

Fees

You should be aware of the transaction fee that is imposed by your broker. A broker usually charges a fee per trade and every time you make a withdrawal. Although this may only involve a small amount, it can quickly add up into a significant amount in the long run.

Promos and bonuses

Brokers usually reward their traders with promos and bonuses. Pay close attention to the terms and conditions before you accept a bonus. For example, a broker may offer you a 50% bonus. But, the drawback is that before you can make a withdrawal, you will have to trade the bonus 35 times, or even more. For most people, they tend to lose their entire bankroll before they even meet the requirement to cash out the bonus/promo. If you think that you cannot satisfy the requirement, then it would be better if you do not accept the bonus.

Deposit and withdrawal limit

It is also suggested that you check the minimum and maximum deposit and withdrawal that is allowed by your broker. This information is usually found on the Banking page. If you cannot find it, do not hesitate to contact your broker.

Required documents

It is not uncommon for brokers to ask for certain documents like valid IDs and proof of billing before they process a withdrawal. Be sure that you have these documents in your possession. Brokers do not usually ask for such documents when you make a deposit, but they usually require them when you make a withdrawal. If you do not have the required documents, contact the customer support team and ask for substitute documents that you can submit to them. Make sure that this part is clear to you before you even make a deposit; otherwise, you will run the risk of having your bitcoins locked in your trading account without any way of withdrawing them.

Demo account

Most reputable brokers will provide you with a demo account. A demo account will allow you to trade bitcoins and other cryptocurrencies in a real and live market without any risk. Of course, you will not earn any real income from it, but you can use the demo account to test your strategy, as well as to familiarize yourself with the actual trading environment. If a demo account is not provided by your broker, what you can do is to open an account with another broker just to take advantage of a demo account. If you want, you can just switch completely to another broker. Another option that you have is simply to trade with very small amounts to minimize your risks.

Do I need a trading broker?

You do not always need a broker to make money with bitcoin. In fact, the only reason why you may want to use a broker is if you intend to trade cryptocurrencies. If you just want to invest in bitcoin, then you do not need to have a broker. Many investors just use their hot wallets to store their bitcoins, and then they sell them after some time for profit. Simply put, if you do not want to trade cryptocurrencies, then you do not need a broker. For the mere purpose of investing in bitcoin, all that you need is a bitcoin wallet.

Chapter 7:

Best Practices

Sufficient research

Make sure that you do enough research before you invest any real money in anything. This is not just about doing a research. You need to be sure to do *sufficient* research. This means that the amount and quality of information that you have should be sufficient to help you come up with a sound investment decision. It is true that no matter how hard you research on something, there is still no guarantee that you will end up with a positive profit; however, do not forget that the more that you know and understand bitcoin, the more likely that you will be able to predict its price movement. Still, remember, there is no 100% guarantee of making a successful trade or investment despite the amount of research that you make. Taking risks is part of the game. If you do sufficient amount of research, then you significantly increase your chances of making a profit.

Bitcoin trading journal

Although not a requirement, having a bitcoin trading journal can be a useful tool. You do not need to be a professional writer to write a journal. You have to update your journal regularly and be completely honest with everything that you write in your journal.

A journal will allow you to see yourself from a new perspective that is free from any form of bias or prejudice. You should make it a habit to update your journal truthfully and regularly for it shall serve as a mirror of yourself as a trader/investor. Ideally, your journal should contain your strategies, objectives, mistakes, and lessons, as well as a record of your trades. Since it is your own personal journal, feel free to record in your journal everything that is related to your activity as a bitcoin investor/trader.

When you read your journal, you will be able to envision yourself from a clearer perspective. Do not hesitate to make adjustments and work on flaws that you may see in your current strategy.

Also, focus on further developing your strengths. Although writing a journal can be quite time-consuming, the benefits and lessons that you can get from it are well worth every effort that you put into your journal.

Money management

How you manage your money is important to your success. Poor money management can cause you to lose all your investment. Therefore, you need to have a plan. A good way to do this is to write down your plan and objectives on a paper or in a notebook. Know how much you are willing to invest in bitcoin, as well as how much profit you expect to make. Make your plans reasonable. Although investing in bitcoin usually gives positive returns, it is still an investment. Therefore, you should also be ready to face some risks. As a rule, you should only invest the money that you can afford to lose. Therefore, do not invest the money that you need to pay for your household bills and other obligations. You should have a plan on how much money you are willing to invest, as well as how you intend to use the bitcoin in your account.

Cryptocurrency

Analyzing expert advice

People who are new to bitcoin usually rely on the pieces of advice given by so-called experts. They usually read their articles, books, and blog posts. The sad truth is that many of these so-called experts are real experts when it comes to making money with bitcoin. Especially in today's age, it is very easy to promote one's self as an expert on social media with just a click of a mouse. Of course, there are also real experts out there, but even these true experts also commit mistakes from time to time. Instead of completely relying on expert advice, what you need to do is to form your own understanding of the bitcoin market. Instead of believing everything that the experts are saying, you should try to examine and analyze their point of view. Remember: Never make any investment simply because an expert has told you to do so. As a beginner, it is good to read as much as you can about bitcoin and visit related blogs and sites. Do not forget that you should develop your own understanding of bitcoin. Not to mention, even the real experts themselves also have conflicting views from time to time.

Take a break

You should give yourself time to take a break and relax from time to time. Remember that you will be more able to think more clearly and objectively if you give yourself time to relax. The best way to relax is to do something that is not related to bitcoin trading and investing. It is also important that you do not think of anything that is related to bitcoin during the time that you are relaxing. This is the best time for you to go on a vacation with your family. After all, being a professional investor can be a busy job; you deserve to enjoy and have fun from time to time. The good thing about this is that your mind will be more refreshed the moment you get back to work, which will allow you to think more clearly and come up with a sound investment decision. As an investor, you have full control of your time. Needless to say, do not abuse this prerogative. Remember that you should take a break to allow you to recover from too much work and not because you are feeling lazy to work.

Withdraw

Many investors and traders do not withdraw their profits on the reasoning that if they do not withdraw their profits, then they will have a bigger fund that they can use for trading/investing. Therefore, the profit potential will also be higher. Although this point is reasonable, it is still important to withdraw and cash out your profits from time to time. After all, you do not have to withdraw all your profits at once. If you want, you can just withdraw 30% of your total profits every week. This is a matter of personal preference, but the important thing is for you to make a withdrawal from time to time. The reason is that no matter how much profit you make, it will not be completely realized until you turn it into cash. To do so, you need to make a withdrawal. Another reason is that making a withdrawal minimizes your losses. Once you withdraw and turn your bitcoins into cash, then they are no longer exposed to the risks that naturally present in a trading environment. If you just come to think of it, if you do not withdraw your profits, then it is almost the same as if you were using a mere demo account. Therefore, do not forget to cash out even just a portion of your overall profits from time to time.

Join groups and forums

Being updated on the news is a good way to receive information about bitcoin. However, news about bitcoin is not limited to what is shown on the news. By joining bitcoin and cryptocurrency groups and forums online, you will be able to get more information. In fact, many updates about bitcoin and other cryptocurrencies first appear in online groups and forums before they turn into news headlines or clips. The reason is that even the developers of many cryptocurrencies are active in online groups and forums. Therefore, if you are serious about making money with bitcoin, then it is strongly suggested that you join and participate in online groups and forums on bitcoin, as well as other cryptocurrency. Another advantage of joining such groups is to learn other interesting ideas and perspectives from other investors and traders.

Test your strategy

Test your strategy several times before you apply it using real money/cryptocurrency. No matter how much you read about a certain strategy, the only way to learn how to apply it properly is by actual application. If you want to be a professional trader, then you should know that working on your strategy is a life-long journey. If you hate continuously developing a strategy, then perhaps being a trader is not for you. Your strategy is an important part of your activities as a trader. You are expected to work on your strategy continuously. Do not forget that bitcoin is highly volatile, and so your strategy should be able to adapt to changes in the environment.

There appears to be no strategy that can work for all types of situations. You need to be flexible enough and adapt to changes. You should also remember that even if you just change a minor part of your strategy, then you should give it a series of tests before applying it using real money. When you are a trader or investor, you should understand that a slight change in a strategy can create a big difference. Therefore, always remember to test your strategy.

Wait it out

Never make decisions when you are under pressure. Also, in case the market is in panic, you should learn to be calm. It is normal for an investment to face some complications or problems from time to time. If the thing where you invested your money in is truly valuable, then it will be able to recover after some time. As an investor, sometimes the best way to face a difficult time is simply to wait it out. If you examine the past trends of bitcoin, you will see that it also faced certain problems, such as when Russia considered it to be illegal. Today, Russia is one of the supporters of bitcoin. If the price of bitcoin drops significantly, many investors begin to panic. You should not be like them. Instead, learn to be patient and understand the real situation. Moreover, during times when you do not know the best move to take, remember that sometimes the best action is simply to wait it out.

Right understanding of high volatility

When people describe bitcoin, one of the things that they will certainly mention is its high volatility. However, what does it really mean when you say that something has a high volatility? Simply put, high volatility only means that the price changes significantly within a short period of time. But, how does it change? Many people think that a drop in price will soon be followed by a high increase in price. Conversely, a high increase in price will soon be followed by a significant decrease in price. It is as if it will balance itself out in the long run. This is not what high volatility is, especially the high volatility of bitcoin. When you deal with bitcoin, you should understand that a series of increase can still follow a high increase in price, and a decrease in price can still be followed by another significant drop in value. You cannot expect the price to balance itself out even in the long run. The price of bitcoin is not something that just comes at random, but it depends on many factors.

Professional approach

There are people who approach bitcoin trading/investing as a hobby. Although there is nothing wrong with this, you should also not expect to get a high amount of profit. If you just want to deal with bitcoin as a mere hobby, a good suggestion is simply for you to follow the buy and hold strategy instead of actively trading bitcoins with other cryptocurrencies. If you trade bitcoins, then you should also have a good understanding of other cryptocurrencies.

If you are serious about making money with bitcoin, then you should approach it professionally. This means that you should be dedicated and committed to it. Usually, people who only take it as a hobby do not exercise enough discipline, and so they fail to make any decent profit. Although there is still no guarantee that you will make a good amount of profit if you approach it professionally, it is certain that following a professional approach can significantly increase your chances of making positive returns. Now, in case that you want to trade bitcoins but simply do not have enough time to study the market, the best suggestion is for you to make just a few trades. When it comes to bitcoin trading and investing, you should never rely completely on luck. Of course, luck can give you profits from time to time, but you cannot expect for it alone to keep you in a positive profit in the long run.

Start small

Even if you have lots of bitcoins in your account, it is good to start small. This is true, especially if you engage in cryptocurrency trading. As a beginner, your first objective is not to make money right away but simply to familiarize yourself with the trading environment. Starting out with a small amount is also a good way to avoid being an emotional trader.

Do not be an emotional trader/investor

Never allow your emotions to dictate your decisions. Being an investor or trader can be a sad life. It is the kind of life where nobody cares even if you lose all your money at once. The market does not care about you; the bitcoin cryptocurrency does not even know you at all. This is the kind of life where everything is purely business without any need for human interaction. The whole process of trading or investing happens online and usually with just a few clicks of a mouse. From then on, all that you need to do is wait and hope for the best.

To avoid being an emotional trader, you should not be attached to your bitcoins. Hence, make sure not to invest the money that you cannot afford to lose. Also, never panic. The moment you notice that you are not thinking clearly, then learn to stop and just relax for a while. Do not make rush decisions. If you want to have any success with cryptocurrency trading, then learn to control yourself, and always make decisions objectively.

Continuous practice

Success in trading or investing in bitcoin is not something that you master simply by reading books. Every true investor/trader knows the importance of continuous practice. You may want to use your broker's demo account to practice. Of course, every actual trade that you make is also part of the practice. Take the time to stop and reflect upon the effects of every transaction that you make.

Chapter 8:

The Future of Bitcoin

Nobody can tell for sure what the future of bitcoin will be. If you look at its past and present trends, it is easy to see that a bright future awaits it. More and more people are being open to the use of bitcoin, as proven by the fact that its price is continuously rising. Today, even governments are taking interest in bitcoin. In some states, you can now pay for your electric and other household bills in bitcoins. In the Philippines, you can convert your bitcoins into cash and enjoy cardless withdrawal at selected ATMs. In other states, you can now book a hotel room and even purchase an airfare ticket online using bitcoin.

Many experts say that the price of bitcoin is expected to reach more than $10,000 for 1 bitcoin in less than two years. Bitcoin is continuously gaining population and attention, and more and more people are drawn to it. In the future, it is expected that banks will have a separate account for bitcoins. Some even claim that bitcoin, as powered by its blockchain, will soon take the place of banks and will take the form of a one-world cryptocurrency. After all, we now live in a computer and Internet generation, and bitcoin is the money of the Internet.

It is not just bitcoin that you should watch out for. Blockchain technology, the backbone technology of bitcoin, is also gaining popularity and worldwide interest. Experts found that this technology is not only applicable to financial services but can also be used for other purposes.

Indeed, the bitcoin revolution is changing the world. Among all the cryptocurrencies in the world, it is only bitcoin that demonstrates a constant positive development. Today, more and more people want to learn about bitcoin. It is this kind of attention and curiosity that works well in favor of bitcoin. Now, it is common for bitcoin users to promote bitcoin on social media. Usually, bitcoin is promoted as a form of a lucrative investment and not just as a substitute for money. After all, bitcoin is, indeed, a lucrative investment. Instead of investing in stocks where a profit of 15% per year is already considered to be high, this 15% can be earned in a few days or even in a single day if you invest in bitcoin.

What the future holds remains a mystery for bitcoin. Although things seem to appear promising for bitcoin, you should not underestimate the fact that there are still risks involved when you deal with bitcoin. There is a possibility that bitcoin may just disappear completely without any warning. Just like any other investment, there is a chance for you to turn bitcoin into a goldmine of profit but there is also a risk that you can lose your investment. The good news is that if you just look at the trend, it is easy to see that bitcoin remains to be a lucrative investment. In fact, you do not even need to do anything complicated. A simple but and hold approach will be enough for you to enjoy profits from your investment in bitcoin. The price of bitcoin is continuously increasing while more and more people are becoming more aware of it and learning about it. Indeed, there are good reasons to believe that the price of bitcoin will constantly increase in the coming months or even years.

Cryptocurrency

The classic example that if you invested even just $500 in bitcoins in 2010, then you would have been a multimillionaire by now remains true even today. Although you may not be a multimillionaire if you just invest $500, the chances are that you can still expect to realize some nice profits.

Bitcoin is the key to financial freedom. The future will depend on what you do today. Merely reading about bitcoin is not enough. For you to enjoy all the benefits and profits that it brings, you need to take positive actions. So, invest in bitcoin today and live a happier and successful life.

Conclusion

Thanks for making it through to the end of this book. We hope it was informative and able to provide you with all of the tools you need to achieve your goals whatever they may be.

The next step is to apply everything that you have learned and start earning real profits by investing in and trading bitcoin. Reading books and articles on the subject is an important step to learning how you can turn bitcoin into a goldmine. However, reading alone is not enough. Another important step that you should take is to apply your knowledge. Since you have reached this part of the book, it is safe to assume that you already have enough knowledge on how you can make money with bitcoins. Remember to observe the teachings in this book, especially the best practices. Unfortunately, some people get too greedy and end up losing their investment. Do not be like them. Again, it bears stressing that if you intend to make serious profits with bitcoin, then you should take it seriously and professionally.

Bitcoin can offer the doors to financial freedom. It is continuously gaining popularity, and people from around the globe are being more open to it. The good news is that this kind of promotion can lead to significant increases in its value. The more people are drawn and get interested in bitcoin, the higher is the probability for its price to take an upward swing.

Although bitcoin is gaining worldwide attention, it is still fairly new in the market. We can still expect some more improvements and developments in the future. That means you have to make sure self prepared for the possible problems that you may encounter with Bitcoin. Remember, the developers of this currency are not perfect, there could be system issues that may occur from time to time. If so, seek help from the professionals. You might want to reach out to the Bitcoin geeks that can help you solve your problems. Nobody knows what Bitcoin will become in the future. No one knows if this new currency will soar high like a bird. But we can be positive about the outcomes. As more and more people use and trust Bitcoin, we can be confident that Bitcoin's future shines as bright as the sun. It is still in the developing process, and as the time passes, more improvements are being implemented.

As an investment, there is no guarantee that investing in bitcoin today will rake in positive profits in the future. Just like any other investment, there is always the risk that you may end up losing your money. The good news is that if you look at the long-term trend of bitcoin, you will easily see that it is progressing positively and that you will most likely earn a nice profit if you stick to it. So far, the price of bitcoin has maintained its upward swing over the years. Of course, it is also subject to the usual fluctuations, but if you observe its long-term behavior, it cannot be denied that its price is taking a positive direction, which makes it a very lucrative investment. Now, is it already too late to invest in bitcoin? Clearly, the answer is *No*. In fact, if you analyze the current trend, you will easily find good reasons to believe that its price will continue to increase over the coming months as more and more people are supporting it.

By now, you should already have enough knowledge and understanding of what bitcoin is really all about. Now, it is time for you to journey and apply everything that you know about bitcoin. After all, knowledge without application is good for nothing.

Again, Bitcoin is not just another toy. It's a real currency that can either make you money or can turn you broke. Gather as much information as you need to fully understand the platform.

Finally, if you found this book useful in anyway, a review on Amazon is always appreciated!

www.ingramcontent.com/pod-product-compliance
Lightning Source LLC
Chambersburg PA
CBHW071251220526
45468CB00001B/84